MOVING.

The What, When, Where, & How of It

Buying, selling, building, renting
a house, condo, or apartment
• Making the physical move
• Understanding contracts
• Obtaining financing
• Reestablishing yourself
• Moving with children

Patricia Obermeier Neuman

To
people everywhere
who are moving anywhere,
with my best wishes;
and to
Rosalind and my parents,
with my deepest gratitude.

MOVING
THE WHAT, WHEN, WHERE, & HOW OF IT

Patricia Obermeier Neuman

ICARUS PRESS

SOUTH BEND, INDIANA

1981

Moving: The What, When, Where, & How of It

Copyright © 1981 by Patricia Obermeier Neuman

Manufactured in the United States of America.

Thanks to Brian Obermeier, Chuck Coppola, Steve Kent, Clayton Obermeier, and Charles Obermeier for sharing their expertise on taxes, law, real estate, financing, and condominiums. And many thanks to Rosalind Coulter for her illustration ideas and to Betty Obermeier and Bruce Fingerhut for their editorial assistance and guidance. And many, many thanks to my husband John (and his employer), without whom I might have never moved!

Icarus Press, Inc.
Post Office Box 1225
South Bend, Indiana 46624

Library of Congress Cataloging in Publication Data
Neuman, Patricia Obermeier, 1947-
   Moving: the what, when, where & how of it.
   Includes index.
   1. Moving, Household—Handbooks, manuals, etc.
I. Title.
TX307.N48   643   81-5059
ISBN 0-89651-450-1   (pbk.)   AACR2

7033762

CONTENTS

1

UPRUTTED, NOT UPROOTED

So your husband came home one day and said, "I have something serious to discuss with you," and you knew he was either going to tell you of an affair he'd been having or of an impending transfer. And you weren't sure which would be worse.

I have been through three such episodes (transfers, luckily, not affairs). I feel that three times is often enough to make me somewhat of an expert at handling a move gracefully. At the same time, I have not moved so often that I have become hardened or have forgotten the pain and agony involved in a relocation. If you are about to embark on your first move, whether to parts unknown or just around the corner, or if you've made other moves that have left you dissatisfied and you now face another move, you have a great challenge ahead of you—but nothing you can't conquer. Take a deep breath, and let's take this one step at a time.

To Move or Not to Move

The first step, and one of the most difficult, is deciding whether or not even to make a move, be it a transfer or your own private venture. When we received our first "offer" from my husband's employer, we had no doubts. When my husband foolishly asked me, "Do you want to move?" I told him immediately and firmly, "No. I'm doing just fine here, where we have lived for nine years, where my parents live, where all our children were born, and where we are very settled and happy, thank you." He agreed.

Almost as soon as we had congratulated ourselves on making the right decision (after all, weren't we saving our children from the trauma of a move? and weren't we wise to stay where we *knew* we liked it instead of taking a chance on a new location?), we began to ask ourselves and each other a few "why nots."

"Why *not* move the kids?" my husband asked me. "Wouldn't it be an invaluable learning situation?" I had to agree. It would be a great experience for them learning to cope with future changes in their lives. And why not get to know another area of the country?

"And why not make some new friends—never forsaking the old, of course, but who is to say they will be staying here anyway?" he asked me. It was true. Joy and Chuck had already left, and Pete and Anna had been talking seriously about moving. We could end up staying, only to watch the rest leave us behind.

"Why not accept the promotion and accompanying financial rewards from the company?" I asked, thinking of the delightful prospect of a new, larger home.

It began to sound more and more like a viable course of action, so we got the kids settled in bed, put on a pot of coffee, and began the first of what would be many lists. This list had two sections: *Advantages of Moving* and *Disadvantages of Moving*. We assigned points to each item listed, on a scale of 1 to 10, depending on how great an advantage or disadvantage it was.

There were many disadvantages to a move, which I won't go into here. I'm sure you will have enough of your own. I will say, though, that they seemed to be based mostly on a reluctance to be uprooted. There were even more *advantages*, we found, and most of them seemed to revolve around a longing to get out of our collective and individual ruts.

We pondered the list for several days, vacillating between a desire to forget the whole thing and a strong urge to move on. It was frustrating at the time that whenever my husband said we should move, I became reluctant. And if I adopted a "let's go" attitude, *he* began to have second thoughts. We finally realized that this devil's advocate syndrome was healthy (if confusing) and enabled us to explore all the possible ramifications of a relocation.

Luckily, my husband had to give his company an answer, or we might still be trying to decide. If that were the case, I would have lost my sanity long ago, as evidenced by this entry from the journal I kept during our first move.

9/17/75

   We just have to arrive at a decision soon. I can't stand this not knowing. I don't feel I can make any commitments or involvements here, since we might be moving. But if we stay, I will have missed out on bowling, a night class, and whatever else might come up while we're trying to make up our boggled minds. I've heard of men without a country, and as dramatic as it may sound, I don't think I feel any less homeless right now than one of them!

I was not the only one to feel this way. Without exception, everyone I have interviewed agreed that *any* decision is better than not knowing. So gather all your facts and thoughts, and do the best you can. And do it quickly!

It would be ideal, of course, if you could visit the new location before you have to make a decision as to whether or not you want to live there. An in-person investigation would be more reliable than the public relations material you might have from the chamber of commerce.

I'm still not quite sure what finally led us to our decision, whether it was the list of advantages and disadvantages or a mental flip of a coin, but we did decide to accept the transfer. If you are reading this book, you too must have decided (for your own good reasons) to move.

Overcoming Early Moving Blues

Now, where to go from here? What do you need to do, and in what order? We felt almost panic-stricken at this point in our first move, but by the third move we just set into motion the system we had employed and perfected during the first two. Nothing could have gone more smoothly.

Before I talk about what *can* go smoothly, though, let me address myself to something that just can't go smoothly for most people moving to a new area, something that only time seems to take care of. Now I sound like I'm talking of death, don't I? Well, the truth is, I couldn't help comparing the psychological stages I went through with each move to the stages I had heard one goes through when one learns of a terminal illness. Let's face it. Moving *is* a death of sorts. It is a death of a life as it *was*. In our case, five lives! Three times!

When my friend Carla called to tell me they were going to have to move, she exhibited all the signs of the first stage. She said, "Patty, I just can't believe it. I truly cannot picture us living in another home, town, or state." I felt this same inability to comprehend each time we were faced with a move situation. In fact, as Carla wrote us after their move, "It takes many months in the new surroundings for the reality of a move to begin to sink in."

After disbelief, I register anger. Why, when things are going so well, did this issue have to erupt to upset our lives? Since our moves have always been job transfers for my husband, my anger has been directed at him and his company. Since I never had the courage to run ranting and raving into his place of business, and since I hardly saw my husband during these times (he always seemed to be working both his old and new positions during the hectic move periods), I had to let my anger out elsewhere—usually in my journal. Great therapy. And cheap!

> *10/1/75*
>
> John came home exhausted again. They still haven't found his replacement. Don't they know he's irreplaceable? I felt a rush of sympathy when he came dragging in the door tonight. But then whose career are we advancing anyway? There surely is a less traumatic way to win a promotion! Damn! I just can't seem to rid myself of all the resentment and ambivalent feelings.

Fortunately for all concerned, my anger has always dissipated quite quickly, but only to be replaced by grief. This is the Crying Stage for me. Once I have shed all the tears my body can manufacture, I am finally able to reach the stage of acceptance. I can accept, if not truly comprehend, the fact that we will indeed be moving.

There is another feeling that has been taking hold and growing throughout all these other emotional stages. This is a feeling of anticipation and adventure. In fact, I have found myself more than once since our moves taking issue with someone who is deploring the way companies move "their" people around. I guess that is one way to look at it, but I for one am grateful for the opportunity to have enjoyed all these adventures at the company's expense.

Now don't expect to go through these stages leaving all bad feelings behind. The bad and sad feelings will be with you off and on, some for only a short while and some for the rest of your life. This, I have learned from my many discussions with other "displaced persons," varies greatly from person to person. There seems to be a direct correlation between the degree and duration of sadness and the length of time lived in a particular place.

This would seem to prove that time will indeed heal your wounds as you become more and more settled in a new area. Of course, this means that the more you *do* fall in love and attain harmony with your new environment, the harder it will be to leave. I've had more hard times leaving than I care to remember, and I still have moments when I just ache to be somewhere or with someone I left behind. I just remind myself that had we never moved (and moved and moved), there would be a lot of somewheres and someones I would not even know. That would be a greater loss yet.

The best advice I can give you for resolving your emotional turmoil is to express your negative feelings—to your mate, a friend, on paper, *anywhere*! Express them, and you will feel better. But then, DO NOT DWELL on them. It is now time to concentrate on the good aspects of the move. Adopt a positive attitude. At this point, you would do well to destroy the list of disadvantages you made and read the list of advantages frequently. You see, so much of the success of your move depends on this positive attitude.

I will never forget my sister-in-law Holly's comment to me when she and my brother Chas made a move long before we had even the remotest idea we would ever be transferred. I asked her, "Isn't it terribly hard to be leaving your parents and the new house you just built? How can you stand it?"

She replied, "I know this is something we should do, so I just look at the good things we are going to instead of thinking of what we are leaving behind." I remembered this wise philosophy years later when we were in the midst of our first move. Whenever I started to feel down, I followed her advice, as you can see from the following excerpt from my journal, written just after we had finally arrived at the decision to move.

9/25/75

It's nice to have it *settled*. Now we can move on (in more ways than one) for better or worse. We really don't feel any more certain today than we did yesterday that we are doing the right thing, but now that the die has been cast we must only look at the good points.

I'm sure Holly won't mind if you too borrow her philosophy.

I have found, having children also involved in our moves, that after telling them how I honestly feel and explaining about mixed emotions and encouraging them to have a good cry if they feel the need, that it is better if they see me only in my "up" moods about the move. I have learned that they are quick to imitate in this area just as they are in so many others. I saw how they became enthusiastic when I did and tearful when I did.

One night at the dinner table I got choked up, not on the food but on the talk of our forthcoming move. Our oldest daughter, Kerri, who was eight years old at the time, said, "Mommy, you're ruining it for me. I felt all happy about the move, and now you've made me sad." That really pointed up the need for a positive attitude in front of the children, and from then on I saved my not-so-positive attitude for my husband, parents, and friends. They, as adults, were better able to handle it. The bonus here is that the "faking" of enthusiasm not only convinced my children, but also me, that moving was the right—and fun—thing to do.

Involving Your Children

Another favor you can do for your children is to let them feel, in every phase of the move in every way possible, that they are part of it and that you not only want but need their suggestions and help. They need to know that you as parents must make the final decisions, but they should be made to feel that you are considering their thoughts and desires in arriving at these decisions.

This was a hard conclusion for me to make, since our kids were involved in and upset by the upheaval caused by our discussions of whether or not to move. I realized that should we decide *not* to move, they would have been unnecessarily upset. But better to risk that than to have them feel left out and unimportant when such a momentous decision is being made.

If you do have school-age children, you should notify their teachers as soon as you know of a move. If teachers are made aware of this, they may be more understanding of any possible school problems caused by this change in your children's lives. Also, the teachers can help prepare them academically for a smooth transition.

It is important to help your children adjust to the idea of a move and to do whatever you can to make it easier for them. Note that I said to do whatever you *can*—not what you can't. We as parents are only human, after all, and should not feel guilty about not doing the impossible. My husband temporarily forgot this in his zeal to make the children happy.

9/20/75

Kerri is finally having moments where she seems to be accepting, if not rejoicing about, the move. John is trying to speed things along for her, and thus we've had our first fight about this move. It all started when, in trying to appease Kerri, he suggested maybe we could get a puppy really soon (i.e., *before* the move). "Then the puppy could move with us," he said.

I sent the kids quickly off to a premature bedtime and tried to point out gently the shortcomings of his idea. "John," I said, "this is not exactly the best time for a new puppy. After all, I'm sure I will have my hands more than full trying to keep a house clean and salable with three children and a husband who thinks clothes go *on*, not *in*, the hamper. What I need the very least right now is a puppy doing its pees and poops all over the house."

By this time, my voice had changed from gentle to an embarrassing screech. It just suddenly seemed that I was being taken advantage of. Here I was, somewhat of a martyr to even be *allowing* this move, and then to have more work heaped on my shoulders! It didn't seem fair. I guess I was just very tired after many near-sleepless nights, and I do have a tendency to overreact (in fact, undergo personality changes) when I am tired.

I tried to get hold of myself. "Dear," I forced myself to say quietly, "don't you think we will all be quite busy enough while we are still here; and after we get moved, don't you think we might all be a bit lonely and at loose ends? Just the perfect remedy might be for everyone to hop in the car and go puppy shopping and then keep happily entertained with the new addition. By the time the newness wears off, the kids will probably be quite adjusted."

Being the reasonable person that he is, John acquiesced. I should have just skipped the whole first part of my argument about "poor overworked me" and sensibly mentioned the latter idea. At any rate, he agreed to be the one to explain to the kids tomorrow that we will be waiting until our arrival in Aberdeen for the new puppy. Luckily (?!), it won't be long, since John has to be working there by November 1. And it's company policy to have the whole family there together. They wouldn't want to do anything to upset us! (If I sound just a bit resentful, Dear Diary, it's only because I am!)

So we escaped that disaster, right? Wrong. The next morning when I looked into those three pairs of excited brown eyes and listened to their eager plans for naming the puppy, I decided I could handle still another pair of brown eyes. Why not inject a little happiness into their lives right now to counteract the sadness they feel at the prospect of leaving here? I didn't know I'd soon be regretting my change of heart, and before I knew what hit me, we had a new addition to the family—Minnie (our souvenir from Minnesota).

Now, let's get moving . . .

CHECKLIST

As Soon as You Hear of Possibility of a Move
If you can, visit new location.
List and weigh advantages and disadvantages of the move.
Discuss possible move with children.

As Soon as Possible
Make your decision.
Notify children's teachers of forthcoming move.
Think positive!

2

WRITE ON!

As soon as we had decided to make each move, I found it quite comforting and oh-so-helpful to start a *Move Notebook*. I immediately organized on paper all that I could and then added to it as the move progressed. If there is anything that can make a move go smoothly, it's proper organization. The best way to keep organized is to *write down* (please, in this hectic time, don't try to rely on your memory) everything pertaining to the move. Also, a *Move File* is needed to keep the many important papers that have a way of surfacing throughout a move.

Lists, which I mentioned before, are always a major part of my notebook. Below is a list (what else?) of the lists I like to have. You will no doubt have others of your own in addition to or instead of these.

1. *Things to Do to This House.* Here I put what we needed to do to the house before we could have it appraised or placed on the market (e.g., clean bathroom closet, paint trim, prune trees). This list was always seemingly endless. After each item on this and most of my lists, I specified a target or deadline date for completion. On this particular list, we also found it helpful to separate my chores from those (few) my husband intended to do.

2. *People to Notify Here.* This list consisted of the people that needed to know we were moving—not my parents
(they had known since the first day when I cried on their
shoulders), and not our good friends (I had told them when
it was still supposed to be a top company secret)—but rather
people such as the church school superintendent (so that she
could be lining up a teacher replacement for me), two appraisers, and real-estate brokers (I'll use *real-estate broker*
and *realtor* interchangeably in this book, although the latter
really denotes a broker associated with the National Association of Realtors [see the glossary at the end of this book]).
This list, like all the lists, will grow and shrink throughout
your move as new tasks become necessary and other ones are
accomplished.

3. *Services to Stop Here.* Examples here are newspapers, milk, and phone. Here too I put a date by each so
that I knew when to stop what. It is imperative on all lists to
cross out or check or somehow indicate that an item has been
taken care of. You will not have time to do anything twice.

4. *Things to Look for in a New Area.* There will be
more about this in Chapter 4, but just be sure you start your
list as soon as you learn of a move to allow maximum time to
think of all the important criteria. You can start with the
things you like about your present area.

5. *Things to Look for in a New House (or
Apartment).* Same as above. This list should cover not only
features you want in a house (fireplace, fourth bedroom),
but also some less obvious things that you will want to check
about a house before buying it. See Chapter 4.

6. *Things to Do When Moved and Bored.* This list was
invented during our first move and turned out to be such
good therapy that I used it in the next two moves too. I was
so busy with the chores and details of the first move that I
found myself constantly telling the kids, my husband, or

myself, "I don't have time to do that right now, though I really would love to. When we're settled, I will." After about the tenth time I had said that, I decided I had better get a list started of all these things or I would find myself settled, bored, and lonely, and not remember that I had wanted to teach Kerri to knit or to play Monopoly with Jack. More about this in Chapter 6.

7. *Services to Start in New Locale.* This list will look pretty much the same as List 3. Don't forget dates, and keep in mind that it is usually easier to do as much as possible *before* the move, as you will be even busier when you first arrive at your destination. Make the arrangements for your new phone service and anything else you can before you move. Frequently, this can be done with a toll-free call; if not, you may want to handle it by mail.

8. *Address-Change Notifications.* You will not be able to complete these, of course, until you have been househunting and *have* a new address. You can, however, get the list ready early in the move process to allow plenty of time to think of all the people, places, and things to notify of your new address. Look for more about this in Chapter 5.

9. *Things to Leave Here.* This list will probably be small but important nevertheless. This too will be discussed more in a later chapter. I will say here that if I had had this list on our first move, I would not have had to waste time and postage mailing our two garage door remote control devices and all the instructions for the appliances to the people who bought our house. That reminds me of another good list, one I have never made but one that was left for me when we made our last move . . .

10. *List for New Owner.* This can include any tips you think could possibly help someone just moving into your house and area. The list I received from the people who sold us their house included such things as the garbage day for

this neighborhood, school bus times, repairmen they had used and liked, date of the last furnace cleaning, babysitters, and even the names and numbers of the dentist and doctors they preferred. It sure beat walking my fingers through the Yellow Pages, and you can be sure that I will make such a list if and when we leave here.

11. *Things to Keep with Us during the Move.* Here when I say *move*, I mean the actual, physical move—on Moving Day. When you first start making your lists, you will probably not believe that this day will ever really arrive. But it will, and when it gets close, you will want to make this list of things that you do not want to go in the truck with the movers. I will give you some suggestions for this list in Chapter 5.

12. *Things to Do.* This is the place for those 1,001 miscellaneous items. Here I list anything I want to do that has not already been placed on another list. This can include such various duties as returning library books or writing thank-you notes for good-bye parties and presents.

13. *Tax Reminders.* You will want to put in your tax file any receipts or details that will facilitate filing your return for the moving year (if you plan it right, you can really complicate matters by stretching your move over the winter months, thus affecting two tax years; two of our moves have found us regretting this type of timing). You may also want to keep a list of things to do or keep pertaining to taxes. More about taxes in Chapter 6.

While we're on the subject of organizing a move, let me recommend that you make it happen as quickly as possible, if you have any choice in the matter. It is important to make the move happen quickly for the same reasons it was important to make a to-move-or-not-to-move decision quickly.

Luckily for us, our moves happened almost too fast. Six weeks from the day we would even hear of such a possibility, we would find ourselves in our new home. Our friends Gary and Roz were not so lucky. They didn't move for six months after the decision to move was made.

"Our lives just seemed to be in limbo for those six months," Roz has told me. "We felt neither here nor there. We didn't feel like we really belonged *here* anymore, and we certainly didn't belong *there* yet." I think that's a natural feeling with any move, but better to feel that way for six weeks than six months!

It's time now to start doing some of those things that so far are only items on a list.

CHECKLIST

Immediately, If Not Sooner
> *Start* Move Notebook *of lists.*
> *Start* Move File.
> *Notify employers, volunteer organizations, or others who depend on you of the impending move.*
> *Keep track of anything and everything that could affect your income taxes.*

3

FOR SALE OR RENT

If you are following my advice to move quickly, then we don't have a second to spare. This is part of the plan—too busy to brood.

If you are renting now, give your landlord immediate notice in writing of your intention to vacate. For your protection, use certified mail with receipt. Usually you are required to give this written notice at least thirty days before you vacate to avoid a breach of lease penalty.

Shaping Up Your House

If you have a home to sell, the first project should be to get it in peak selling condition. We have learned (the hard way, of course) to keep our home always in this condition. Take a look at the entry I made in my journal during the time we were scurrying to get our home ready for sale.

9/28/75

We are busy doing the things that we hope will bring us top dollar in the shortest time. But we're taking time to write on our "List of Lessons Learned" to always spend

the time and money to do necessary fixing-up and repair-
ing as soon as they need to be done. Otherwise, we'll keep
finding ourselves doing this work in order to sell, when
for the same amount of time and money, it could have
been done earlier (and more leisurely!) for *us* to enjoy—not
some strangers who will soon be invading the premises.

At this point, even if it is for someone else, what needs to
be done must be done. Your time and money probably could
not be invested any more wisely, as the most minor improvements will not only help sell a house, but sell it at a higher
price. Keep all receipts because the IRS will let you deduct
(on Form 2119) fixing-up expenses (for decorating and
repair to assist the sale of a house) incurred within ninety
days before the contract to sell the house is signed (and paid
for not later than thirty days after the sale). See Chapter 6.

As you are preparing your list of what needs to be done,
walk around and through your house, trying all the while to
look at it through the eyes of someone seeing it for the first
time. This is difficult to do but very important. You may be
surprised to find many flaws you have been overlooking for
years that now seem to be glaring.

You will want to make a good first impression on prospective buyers, so put at the top of the list anything that needs
to be done to the yard or the exterior of your home. A fresh
coat of paint (maybe just the trim) can do wonders for the
appearance of a home. See if yours needs it. Maybe it could
at least use a good washing, especially the doors. Make sure
your roof, gutters, mailbox, and driveway are in good repair.
Your yard must be in shape for scrutiny, whether this means
mowing the grass and planting flowers or shoveling snow
from the walks. Many a house has been sold because of a
choice, attractive lot.

Now let's go inside your house and see what can be done
to hasten its sale and fatten your wallet. You may need to

paint some walls, or here again a good washing may suffice. If you do decide to paint, choose a conventional color such as white, off-white, or a pastel that would be easy to decorate around. This will assure you of appealing to a greater number of potential buyers.

One of the small but important things that must be done is the cleaning of cupboards and closets throughout the house. This will serve an additional purpose. If you clean them judiciously (now admit it, you haven't worn that old blue sweater for three years), it will mean less to move, less to unpack when you get to your destination, and more room to store the things you *do* use and wear.

While you're at it, if time permits, you should go through all dresser and other furniture drawers. No, no one will (or should!) look in these when viewing your house, but it would be a good time to accomplish this project while your cleaning-out/throwing-away momentum is up. The less you move, the less it will cost you.

Also, store, throw away, or otherwise remove any items (from furniture to toys) that really are not needed or that do not enhance the visual appeal of your home. A cluttered house is a small house, or so your prospective buyers will think.

Marvine, a nomadic young mother married to a successful pharmaceutical salesman, told me, "Our daughter Rebecca's room is normally filled with her play kitchen set, blackboard, school desk, and whatever else is important to her at the time. When we get ready to sell a house, though, we put as many of these items as we can in the attic (or, if we can talk her into it, the garbage). This makes her room appear neater and larger. Any dismay she feels at saying a temporary good-bye to her favorite possessions put in storage is more than overcome when, on arrival at our new home, she is reunited with them. It's just like Christmas for her—and at a time when such a boost is needed too." I bet most rooms in most houses could benefit from at least a little weeding out. And don't forget to eliminate the clutter from kitchen countertops and bathroom vanities.

My neighbor Jeanne, who has bought and sold even more houses than we have, says, "You must have clean carpets and windows." You should set aside the time or money to follow her advice. The clean windows are especially important if you are depending on a good view to help sell your house.

Jeanne also has found that many people are either turned on or off by the woodwork of a home. "I don't recommend that your readers install new woodwork or even refinish the old, but they can very easily keep what they have polished nicely throughout the selling period," she told me.

It is important to have your bathrooms sparkling clean. Also, make sure there are no leaks or running toilets or clogged drains. Check all the doors in the house, lubricating any that squeak. If you have a door that sticks, rub the surface with a block of paraffin or a bar of soap. The tracks of sliding doors should be clean. If your basement is dark and dreary, paint the walls and ceiling a light color. If you have a musty odor in the basement (or elsewhere), use a room deodorizer.

There may be some areas that you feel need fixing up but that involve such major expenditures that you're not sure it would be worth it. It is true that you should not make major changes unless they increase the value of your property more than the cost of the improvement.

The Appraisal

When you have readied your house for sale, now and only now should you have it appraised. Don't rely, especially in the current market, on your purchase price or a friend's well-meaning advice to arrive at a selling price. An appraiser that belongs to one of the professional organizations such as the Society of Real Estate Appraisers (SRA) or the American Society of Appraisers (ASA) can best guide you. If you can spare the money, two appraisals would give you an even better guide.

Point out to the appraisers, and any realtors who may become involved later, any items that will remain and any items that you plan to take with you. This will insure a more accurate evaluation of your house. I think it is advantageous to the seller, in the long run, to include draperies and curtains (which usually won't fit in your new house anyway) and appliances in the sale of the house. Also, point out to the appraisers and realtors any improvements you have made, but don't count on *misplaced* improvements to raise the price.

Be careful, when setting the asking price for your home, not to give it away and also not to price yourself right out of the competition. Pricing a house right means pricing it on the neighborhood scale. Take care to price it right. This, of course, was the reason for the appraisal. Be sure to leave room for negotiation—in other words, ask *more* than you expect to get—if such is the usual practice in your area.

Selling It Yourself or Listing with a Realtor?

Next you will have to decide whether to try to sell the house yourself or list with a realtor. If you are not pressed for time, or if you have an employer backing you, it can't hurt to try yourself for at least a brief period. Two weeks should give you a fair idea of how much action you can generate yourself. You won't have much to lose and maybe about 7 percent to gain. You will have to be willing to spend some money on advertising in the newspapers (keep track of such expenses for tax purposes). Another good investment is a *For Sale* sign (keep that receipt too), preferably one similar in size and shape to those used by realty companies, since it will attract more attention than a smaller version.

If you decide to list with a realtor, you will want to choose one with the utmost care. Have two or more realtors come to discuss their listing proposals and to give you a realtor's opinion of your home's market value. You should also discuss selling expenses and the various types of sales and financial plans that can affect your net realized selling price.

In selecting a realtor, ask around for recommendations from people who have had recent experience with one. Lacking that, look for a realtor whose signs you see frequently in your area (with *sold* added to them, of course). If these two methods do not produce names of realtors for you, go with one affiliated with a well-known company. Make sure the realtor you select is a member of a multi-listing service. This will give your house the greatest possible exposure.

It will be more expedient to have a realtor whose office is located near your home. There may be many times you will want to check on the progress in person, which you should do, and this will be easier if you don't have to drive forty-five miles away. In addition, it pays to have a realtor who is familiar with your area, and this is more apt to be true if his/her office is located nearby.

Choose a realtor who seems to be organized, efficient, and assertive. The realtor should tell you what your competition is and what comparable homes in your vicinity are selling for. It is probably not wise to list with a realtor who is also trying to sell his/her own home.

When you have chosen the realtor you feel is best for your needs, make sure the listing agreement you sign specifies the period of time that the listing is in effect, the asking price, the realtor's commission rate, and any exclusions you wish to make regarding potential buyers you may already have. Maybe Uncle Fred is still considering buying your house. You can't wait forever for him to make up his mind, yet should he decide to buy, you don't want the realtor to get the commission. So exclude Uncle Fred in the listing agreement.

Do not list your home for longer than sixty days. This will give you the opportunity to change realtors if you are disenchanted with the first one. If you do like the way he/she has been operating, you can always extend the listing period.

Do not let the realtor include in the listing any extra fees for advertising or other costs. Also, refuse to enter into an agreement that stipulates a commission payment even if a prospective buyer backs out before closing. You should not have to pay your realtor anything until closing.

I suggest that the listing agreement should not exclude GI or FHA buyers, since you would be limiting your market. (See more about GI—also known as VA, or Veterans' Administration—and FHA loans in the next chapter.) If you fear that selling your house to someone who finances with one of these government-insured loans would cost you, as the seller, more in closing costs, then raise the selling price enough to cover this added expense. Then, if you get a buyer who is going to obtain a conventional loan, which is not government insured and which would not require you to pay as much in closing costs, you can lower the asking price accordingly to make the sale.

If you do list with a realtor, you will want to make all appointments and negotiations for the sale of your property through him (it is too cumbersome to keep saying him/her or she/he, so let us assume that the realtor you have chosen is a male). This does not mean, however, that you are relinquishing all rights.

One of your rights is having the final say on the asking price. Remember that the realtor is making his money on the 7 percent commission, and 7 percent of $100,000 is almost as much as 7 percent of $110,000. To you, however, that extra $10,000 amounts to a lot. Don't let him talk you into a price that is lower than you know is realistic (here the appraisal you had will be worth whatever you paid for it) just so that he can make a quick sale or profit. By the same token, some realtors may tell you they can sell your home at a fantastically high price just to convince you that you should list with them. Beware!

Let me hasten to say, lest I give the wrong impression, that I do not wish to imply that realtors are not to be trusted. On the contrary, our dealings with various realtors have left us with great respect for the profession. But like all professions (including writing), there are those who are scrupulous and those who are unscrupulous. I don't need to warn you about the good ones, who are worth their weight in gold. It will be those few "others" that I will have to mention from time to time. With so much at stake, I just want you to be adequately informed, since it is *you* who has to accept the ultimate responsibility for every facet of your move.

You also have the right to receive monthly reports of just what your realtor has done in the way of advertising and showing your home. It is a normal practice for a realtor to leave a business card every time he has shown your house, but it is nice to see it all in one complete report every month.

Showing Your House

I do not recommend open houses—they just don't seem to be worth the effort. A realtor even told us once (yes, we've used realtors—you can't always sell a house yourself; in our case, you can't *ever* sell a house yourself) that open houses usually attract curiosity seekers or people who are actually looking for a house in a lower price bracket. If your house is well advertised in the paper, anyone who wants to see it will notice the ad and make arrangements. Many people drive around areas they like looking for houses that may be for sale, so your yard sign will be a good advertisement too. One more word about open houses from my friend Roz. "Another drawback," she says, "is that you run out of places to go and things to do on a Sunday afternoon."

When showing your home, make sure your rooms are adequately lit. Replace any burned-out light bulbs, and wash the bugs and dust off light fixtures. You may even want to use larger light bulbs than you normally do to make your home brighter. Keeping the draperies and shades open will help brighten your rooms, as well as make them seem larger. Turn on all the inside lights before a showing, and if it's dark, turn on the outside lights also.

A little atmosphere, via flowers, soft music, and a fire in the fireplace (unless it's a sweltering August afternoon) is nice. Even such a simple thing as putting out fresh towels in the bathroom makes your home more appealing. In other words, use all the special touches you would for an important guest. Whoever buys your house will certainly be important to you!

As much as I love kids and dogs in a home I live in, they are not assets to a house that is being shown. Let me illustrate with a sad-but-true story.

10/9/75

I knew we shouldn't get that damn dog! Lee and Pam came this morning and we visited while the kids played. Of course, we didn't worry about the house—didn't want to waste a single minute of one of our last times together. We figured if the realtor called to show the house, the three of us could whip it in shape in no time. Unfortunately, we didn't consider the possibility that the realtor would break her promise to phone first. We were flustered and humiliated when she just appeared at the door with a prospective buyer. They took one quick glance at the wall-to-wall cover of toys, cookie crumbs, shoes, coats, and well, you name it, it was probably there somewhere, and left.

I was in shock. After two weeks of having a spotless house and NO one coming to see it, the first time I finally let my guard down, someone comes. The absolute topper, no doubt the reason the realtor and her client were out of the door almost before they were even in, was the contribution of Minnie's I found in the corner of the living room—the one room I *thought* was clean. I'm not sure whether to call the realtor and apologize for the mess or tell her what I think of her for not calling first. I suppose she figured since the house was immaculate just yesterday when she stopped by for me to sign those papers that it couldn't be much different today. Well, then she must not have children! And certainly not a new puppy!

If it is a realtor who will be showing your home, it would be best if your entire family left the house. Buyers are more relaxed and more apt to take their time to really consider a home if they don't feel the owners are watching their every move.

Have a clear understanding with your realtor as to how much advance notice you want before the house is shown. You will want to be quite flexible and accommodating in this so that you don't pass up any potential customers who may have only a couple of days in town to buy a house.

Our policy has always been to ask that the realtor give us as much notice as possible, but that if he is unable to reach us to go ahead and show the house. We made sure never to leave the house unless it was reasonably showable. Only once did this failsafe method fail us, but you already know that sordid story. Once is too often, so I advise you that when you have your house for sale, keep in mind that someone might want to look at it at any minute. Always be ready!

By always being ready, I do not mean that you should have your house picture-perfect every second, thereby driving your family and yourself crazy. In fact, among my circle of also-transferred friends, there are some who say that whenever they are househunting, they don't really take into consideration whether or not a house is clean or picked up. They feel they are able to look around and through any dirt and clutter to discern the basic floor plan and visualize how it would look if they moved in.

Others tell me, and I find this to be true for me, that they aren't able to picture much in their minds and, therefore, always ended up buying homes that were impressive to look at. (This, I know, can sometimes be a mistake. I feel we have passed up some run-down places we could have got at bargain prices and fixed up for a profit. Instead, we have always bought houses that are already to our liking. This has definite advantages, though, when you move as frequently as we do.)

My former neighbor Sue told me, "I judge the *un*seen parts of the house by how neat and tidy I find the *seen* parts, assuming that the owners probably take care of the entire dwelling in the same manner." I guess this is one criteria to use, but I think it may prove too often fallible. Some people *do* spend the money on the "important" things (upkeep on appliances and necessary repairs) but just don't put "polish refrigerator" high on their list of priorities.

Just to play it safe, though, not knowing which type of "customer" may call on you, do keep your house reasonably cleaned and reasonably picked up. (And, please, no dog poop on the floor.) It will sell more easily that way. And just think. Maybe your family will establish some good housekeeping habits that will carry over to your new home when you move.

I must admit that this pressure of keeping a house constantly in order is the least favorite part of a move for me, probably because it is so against my nature. For this reason, I always wanted our houses to sell quickly. Thus far luck has not been with me—two of our houses sold the day before we moved and the third sold *after* we had moved. I always wondered wistfully what it would be like to be able to relax the last month or so before a move and just visit with loved ones we'd soon be leaving, instead of constantly worrying about the condition of the kitchen or whether or not Jack had flushed the toilet. Maybe if there's a next time, I'll get my chance to find out. After all, the law of averages should be on my side.

O Lord, How Long?

Please do not panic or fly into a rage or sink into a depression if your house does not sell as quickly as you may have hoped. I remember the letter I got from my friend Betty a month after their house was listed on the market. "Why, oh why, hasn't our house sold?" she implored, having expected it to take only a week or two. And yes, we've all heard the stories of people who have sold their house almost before they even knew themselves it was for sale. Chances are, these stories are greatly exaggerated, most likely by a realtor who is hoping to get a listing.

More often than not, it takes a little longer than that for a house to sell. If it has been longer than ninety days, though, you might ask yourself or your realtor if there is some problem with the house that could be corrected or if you have the house priced too high. If your home is priced above the competition, it won't sell. Remember, the value of your home is determined chiefly by location, neighborhood, and current market conditions.

When an overpriced house has remained on the market

for ninety days, it becomes very difficult to sell. A salesman loses his enthusiasm—easily remedied by changing salesmen. But, not so easily remedied, prospects begin to wonder what is wrong with the house.

At any given moment during the period you are trying to sell, you will have to consider lowering the price if you are eager to move, even if you don't feel it is priced too high. Only you can decide, based on your individual circumstances, just how much you are willing to pay (in terms of lowering the price) for a quick sale. If you have a job waiting for you in a distant city that means a big raise, then certainly you will be willing to take a loss on the house rather than pass up the long-term benefits of your new job. On the other hand, if you are in no great hurry to move, and maybe can't even afford to do so if you don't get the price you're asking for your house, then it would be foolish on your part to lower the price below what the market will bear.

No matter when you sell your house, it is a matter of the right person coming along. After our own three selling experiences, as well as many, many shared with friends and business acquaintances, I can assure you there is someone somewhere looking for a house just like yours. It may take a week, but more likely it will take a couple of months.

The time of year also has a great deal to do with the length of time your home will stay on the market. Naturally, one that is listed in May, all other things being equal, will be more apt to sell quickly than one listed during the Christmas holidays. Our second house was listed for sale in mid-October and didn't sell until March 1. For all the people who came and looked, it might just as well not even have been listed during December, January, and most of February. But it *did* sell. Yours will too.

What to Do with That Offer

When you do get an offer for your home (and remember, you will), there are many things to consider. For one thing, if you are dealing with someone who is having trouble getting a down payment or arranging financing, you will have to decide whether or not you need all the cash out of your home right now. If not, you may be able to carry the buyer's contract or offer him a lease with option to buy or some other alternative to enable him to buy—and you to sell—your property. We will talk about various forms of financing in the next chapter.

You will probably want to have an attorney, especially if you are selling your house "by owner" or if you are entering into a complicated financial arrangement with the buyer.

With or without an attorney, only firm offers *in writing* should be considered. The offer should be submitted on a standard earnest-money contract or purchase-agreement form and should specify the purchase price, terms under which the buyer proposes to buy, down payment, type of financing, closing date, possession date, who pays the taxes (if this is negotiable in your state), and any nonrealty items to be included in the sale (e.g., refrigerator).

Do not accept a promissory note in lieu of earnest money, and be sure to demand enough earnest money to insure that your buyers *are* earnest. Also, set the closing date for the reasonably near future (thirty days is excellent). "We once set it for three months from the date we accepted an offer, only to learn two days before closing that our buyers wanted to back out," lamented Jeanne. Her husband Bill explained, "Apparently they could afford to forfeit the earnest money, most of which went to the realtor, not us, for expenses. To add salt to the wound, we had had the house off the market for ninety days of prime selling time and now had to start all over. That hurt!"

When reaching an agreement with your buyers, avoid any unreasonable contingencies (such as the sale being contingent on them selling *their* house). You may negotiate as to whether or not pending assessments will be assumed by the buyer with conventional financing. If it is a GI or FHA offer, the contract should state the maximum number of points you will pay. (Points represent the amount paid to the lending institution for making the loan. One point equals 1 percent of the mortgage.) If you have already moved or are otherwise accepting an offer from out-of-town, send a wire stating that you accept their offer *subject to review of written contract.*

Not only will the earnest-money contract specify closing date but perhaps where the closing is to be held. Usually, at the closing, you execute a deed, which transfers your interest in the property to the buyer. Your mortgage holder releases you from your obligation after the outstanding mortgage is paid.

Taxes due and payable at the time of closing are usually paid by you, the seller, at closing. Any other outstanding encumbrances, including your outstanding mortgage, must also be paid. You may also have to pay some transfer charges and title-insurance premium (for a policy that insures that the title to the property is clear). Your attorney, escrow agent, or title-insurance company will attest to the fact that the title is clear. And you will have to pay any realtor's commission and attorney's fee at the time of closing. It is not necessary for you to come up with any money at the time of closing, however, as all these costs are taken out of your equity. The net proceeds will be paid to you with a cashier's check.

We have never been present at the closing of any of the houses we have sold. A little planning ahead, to allow time to accomplish it through the mail, was all that was required of us. Another alternative is *power of attorney*, authorizing someone else to act in your behalf.

You should not allow buyers to move in before the closing. If you feel you must because of extenuating circumstances, have your attorney draw up a rental agreement so that you are protected. Be sure to charge at least enough to cover all your expenses on the house.

After you have closed, remember to cancel your household insurance on that residence effective the date of closing so that you can get the refund due you. If you have moved out of the house before selling it, you should have converted this insurance to "unoccupied dwelling" coverage. Also, have the utilities put in the name of the new owner as of the date of closing and have a final bill sent to you.

This pretty much winds things up on this end, so let's find you a new home!

CHECKLIST

Immediately
> *If renting, give notice.*
> *If selling, ready house for sale.*

As Soon as Possible
> *Have house appraised.*
> *Get realtors' opinions and, if desired, list with realtor of your choice.*

When You Receive an Offer
> *Engage the services of an attorney.*
> *Have standard earnest-money contract signed.*
> *Notify your present mortgagee, if necessary.*

Upon Closing Sale of House

Turn over appliance instructions, keys, garage-door-
opener devices, warranties, etc., to new owners.

Cancel household insurance, and obtain any refund due
you.

Switch electric, gas, water, etc., services to name of new
owner and ask for final bill.

Celebrate!

4

HOUSE WANTED

I have read much in favor of parents getting away for a few days without the kids. Believe me, at no time is this more necessary than when it comes to househunting. I don't care *what* I said earlier about involving the children in your move. There is a time and place for everything, and househunting is not the time or place for kids!

Househunting with the Kids—a Distinct Mistake

When we accepted our third transfer and were ready to go on a week's househunting trip, my husband said, "Maybe since it's only 180 miles away, we should drive this time and take the kids along. They would probably enjoy a little vacation from school."

"That's a good idea, hon," I said.

So we took the kids with us, which only goes to prove that by our third move we were still making some mistakes. Never again, no matter how they might plead and beg, will our kids accompany us on a househunting trip. And I feel certain that no matter how much *we* might plead and beg, they would not want to accompany us.

We found that if they weren't complaining about being cooped up in the car, they were flopping on the furniture in a home we were viewing or intruding on a deep conversation my husband and I were having.

"Do you think we could assume that mortgage?" I would ask my husband.

"I want the house on the pond," our son Jack would interrupt.

"We can't get that one," Kerri would say. "It only has three bedrooms, and Mom and Dad promised I'd have my own bedroom this time."

"I want the one with the purple walls," Melissa would put in her two cents' worth.

"What did you say, dear?" my husband would ask me.

"I forgot."

And on and on.

We couldn't help but remember how much better our two previous househunting trips (sans children) had gone. My husband and I felt the same confusion in our own minds on those trips, but at least the kids only knew about the house we finally bought. Of course, we stressed only the positive aspects of it, not telling them that we passed up a house two doors down from their cousins Brad and Scott or that we came close to getting a house with a pool. We took pictures of the "new house" inside and out, as well as pictures of their new school. They were thrilled and excited! They didn't have to concern themselves with whether or not we made the best decision. Their dad and I shouldered that burden.

How to Househunt

Househunting (when we don't take the kids along) is probably the most fun part of a move for me. In fact, in a couple of moves, it was my only salvation. Had I not had the thought of a new house to look forward to, the thought of a move would have been totally unbearable instead of just *almost* unbearable.

At the same time, though, I always find househunting mentally and physically exhausting, and by the time we reach the conclusion of a househunting trip (the formal written agreement), I find myself at the edge of depression. I think this is caused by the fear that we have

a. bought something we simply cannot afford;
b. bought something that will begin to fall apart the day we move in; or
c. all of the above.

I am happy to report that, after having bought four houses, these fears have proved groundless.

Those of you who are moving out-of-town should subscribe to the Sunday edition of a major newspaper in the new location the minute you learn of a move. This will enable you to study the want ads and get a quick fix on homes available there and the price range.

From the papers, you can pick at least two realty companies that seem to be well established there and write to them requesting that they keep their eyes open for you for the type of area and house you want. If you know someone in your new area, you may prefer to have them recommend a couple of realtors, or maybe you know a realtor in your present location who can refer you to someone. Remember, it will cost you nothing as a buyer to use the services of a realtor; the seller pays the commission.

Wherever you get the names of realtors, make sure they are part of a multiple listing service. Through MLS, you will have photographs and detailed descriptions of homes for sale at your disposal, regardless of which realtor or realty company originally listed them.

When you write to the realtors, send them a list of specifics you are looking for, telling them what are musts and what are simply preferences. Let them know what price range you would like to look in and how flexible you are.

From our experiences, I would have to recommend that you be brave in setting your price limit. Our only mistakes in this regard have been to *under*spend. We have been guilty of buying what we could afford to spend at the moment, forgetting that our income would be increasing as my husband's career progressed. Another point to remember is that unless there is a drastic change, your money could probably not be invested any more profitably, so it may be worth a little scrimping to put more money into your home. Besides, how many investments can you enjoy as much as your house?

Ask the realtors to send you information regarding the city, its park district programs, maps, and anything else available. If they don't have their own welcome kits, they can have the local chamber of commerce send you literature. The realtors can also send you listings of available houses to study before your arrival in the new area. I would recommend that you make arrangements to spend time with at least two different realtors when you are in your new city for your major househunting trip.

Narrowing the Field

I say *major* househunting trip because it is an enormous help, if proximity, time, and money allow, to take at least one scouting trip to the new city or town prior to the trip you take for the actual purchase. On such a scouting trip, try to limit yourself to narrowing the field to a particular area or two rather than actually looking at houses.

The importance of choosing an area that fits your needs is

not to be underestimated. Experience has taught me that no matter how much I am depending on the purchase of a near-dream house to pacify me, it is even more important to shop for a dream area. If you are one who thrives on being with people day in and day out, or if you need to be within walking distance of stores and libraries, you obviously will not be happy on six acres fifty miles from civilization, no matter how much you might love the kitchen or the beautiful deck.

Our last move really proved the merit of this theory, when we passed up a larger home with a lower price tag and paid the premium to live on a lake in an area that also has its own pool and tennis courts and oodles of kids. We have never before made such a fast adjustment. We are right in our element. I soon forgot that we didn't have the basement or playroom that we had once enjoyed. Besides, as is always the case, our new house has other attractive features that our previous homes lacked (like the fourth bedroom Kerri wanted).

If you have children, you will want to take into consideration the school district of an area as well as the mode of transportation to and from the schools. Try to spend some time visiting the school(s) in the area in which you think you might want to live. Not only can this help you decide if this will be a good place for your children to be receiving their education, but observing the children there will also give you a true picture of the neighborhood. After all, children do reflect the homes from which they come.

You should check into what activities are available for children (little league, dancing studios, or whatever their interests). You will probably want to rule out areas with busy streets if you have children . . . and maybe even if you don't! Then again, hustle and bustle may be just what you're looking for. Something that is a little harder to discern (but, oh! what a difference it can make) is whether or not an area is made up mostly of people of your age group and whether or not it has a lot of children. Do some investigating.

Visit the local chamber of commerce or city zoning board or planning commission and find out about any long- or short-range developments for any area in which you might be interested. This is especially important if you are considering an area that is just being developed or that is surrounded by open land. Ask about restrictions that might be placed on a home in initial or later zoning requirements. You don't want to invest in a property with the idea of turning it into a duplex if that would be prohibited. Conversely, you might not want to buy in an area that is or will be zoned for multiple-family housing or commercial real estate.

Once you have decided on the area or several areas in which you feel you would be happy, whether on a previous trip or in the first day of your one and only househunting trip, you can limit yourself to the particular area(s) and scour thoroughly in search of the best available house for your needs and money. By the way, be sure you and/or your spouse have taken advantage of any business trips to the new locale to check out any possible "buys."

Believe it or not, my new friend Bonnie even told me, "My husband Ron bought our house before I even looked at it!" I was amazed until I learned that they had been on five househunting trips together in as many years. Obviously, after all that, he knew what she would and wouldn't like. Also, she was protected by a contingency in the earnest-money contract that stipulated that she had the right to view and approve the house within seven days—which she did.

On each and every one of our househunting trips, I have found every feature I have wanted in a house. I can even say that I have *had* every feature in a house that I would want. Unfortunately, the features have never all been in the same house. I have decided, in fact, that I couldn't have everything I want in one house even if we were to build,

because some of the features I want are incompatible with
each other.

Your list of *Things to Look for in a New House or Apartment* will be invaluable to you when it comes to choosing a
house. It will help you keep your priorities in perspective,
especially if you have the features listed in order of importance. Use the list only as a guideline, however, and keep an
open mind. Be flexible, or you will be disappointed. Those of
you who are buying a house in a day or two—even a month
or two—will find it completely different from those of you
who are planning to move into another house in the same
area and can leisurely wait for the right buy to present itself.
(Don't you wish it were that easy?) You must remember that
the less time you have for househunting, the more com-
promises you are probably going to have to make.

For those of you who *are* only changing houses and not
areas, your work should be easier (which is not to say easy)
every step of the way. Since you already live in the area, you
will not need to check into schools, park district programs,
and the like. You're obviously satisfied if you're planning to
stay in the area. Your biggest headache is apt to be timing the
sale and closing of your old residence as closely as possible to
the purchase and closing of your new one to avoid taking
out another loan—a swing loan—and (ouch) double house
payments. Therefore, you will have to decide, depending on
your financial resources and your urgency to move to a different house, whether you want to wait until you find your
dream house before trying to sell your present one, or
whether you first want to make sure this one *is* sold before
committing to a financial obligation on a new one.

When shopping for a house, remember that many things
you might not like about a particular house can be changed.
Don't insist on buying a home with a fireplace. You can
always have one put in. Or can you? Better check for
feasibility.

Another point to keep in mind is that you don't want to find yourself paying for something you don't really care to have. If you buy a house that has a triple garage when you only need a double, then you are paying for something you don't want. Granted, sometimes this is unavoidable, especially when your househunting time is limited.

Something else that may not be on your list but which you should consider when choosing a house, especially if you think you may have to resell someday, is that it is unwise to buy the nicest or most expensive house in an area. It is better to buy a house that is surrounded by homes of equal or higher value. This will make it much easier to resell.

Similarly, it is unwise to buy a house with any outlandish characteristics or abnormalities, even if *you* kind of like them, if you think you may have to resell the house someday. If you plan to be on the move again, better stick with the more traditional so as not to limit your market. Remember, a lot of people would not want a sunken, heart-shaped bathtub, even if you do think it would improve your sex life.

Asking the Right Questions

When you have the houses you are considering narrowed to a manageable number (three or four), you can really start digging for information that will lead you to your best buy. Be sure to find out who the builder was and what kind of reputation he has. Steer clear of any fly-by-night builders or do-it-yourselfers. You will be lucky if you are working with a realtor you feel you can really trust. At this point, let me stress that you should definitely rely on any acquaintances, friends, relatives, or business associates you may know in the new location for recommendations of realtors, attorneys, builders, banks, etc.

Find out how long a house has been on the market. This may or may not be indicative of the quality of the house and neighborhood, but at least you should know if it has been for sale for an unusually long time. If it has, you will want to try to find out why. You can also use this information to enter a lower-than-usual bid, since you can assume that the buyer must either be anxious by now or else he has it overpriced to begin with, since it hasn't sold.

Also, find out what nearby houses of comparable size and quality have sold for in the very recent past. You can ask a realtor to show you listings and other records, and you can ask to see the appraisal of the home you are considering. The appraisal (if it is a thorough one) will show pictures and prices of comparable homes recently sold in an area. If a realtor or owner refuses to show you the appraisal, I would wonder why. Overpriced would be my first guess.

Check any house you are considering for signs of water problems—water marks, musty odor, shrunken or stained carpets. Having lived in a house that became navigable with every rain, I cannot be too emphatic about this. Check for signs that indicate whether the builder did his work the cheapest possible way, or whether he went that extra mile? This can be an indicator as to how the less-visible parts of the house have been built. If he put in a low-grade floor covering, perhaps he also skimped on the plumbing or wiring materials.

In this day and age, it is probably unnecessary to remind you to check for adequate insulation. So enough said on that. Well, one more thing. Ask to see the previous winter's heating bills. Pay special attention to the furnace, especially if the house is not new. Try operating the furnace. Even though this is not a final test, you can at least tell whether it operates quietly and the heat comes up quickly. The furnace should be accessible for service so that it will not be difficult to correct any problems that may arise. If you have any doubts about the furnace in the house you are going to buy, have a qualified person go over the heating system carefully.

Even if there is not enough cupboard and closet space (is there ever?), decide if you think there is enough for you to live with or, if not, if there is any way you could expand on what is there.

It is a good idea to have the house checked for termites, especially if you see signs of the critters in the form of little tunnels in the wood of porches, outside steps, and dark, damp places close to the ground. If there is a problem, and you still want the house, you will want to have them eliminated with the cost, as well as any cost for necessary structural repairs, absorbed by the seller, not you. Ask for a warranty against damages and infestation. Also, look for signs of recent treatment for termites. These would be small, covered holes in the ground or inside in the basement near the wall, indicating that a chemical poison has been injected. You would want a warranty in this case too. Check for signs of other vermin.

Check the amount of real estate taxes you would have to pay annually on any house you are considering. It may make the difference as to whether or not you can afford it.

Do the window appointments stay? Mirrors? Porch swing? Everything you expect to stay would have to be listed in any formal agreement you sign in order to eliminate disagreements and legal entanglements at closing. Our friend Brian goes so far as to recommend taking pictures, since items he felt were too attached to necessitate listing in the earnest-money contract were removed by the seller, leaving him very disappointed in the purchase of his last home.

Your own list of things to check into may consist of entirely different points. Just be sure you do have your list so that you can check for everything while you are there and before you enter into a formal agreement. This is not the time to rely on memory and return home, five hundred miles away, only to ask yourself, "Did that house we bought have a sump pump?"

I have never got a really good feel for a new area until we have moved in and I have driven to the grocery store or schools or any of my other hangouts on my own. This can be too late! Whatever you do, do not decide on an area or house until you have driven around and by it *on your own* enough to really have it in proper perspective in relation to the surrounding town, city, and whatever else may be nearby (airport? dump?). Do not rely on your realtor to point out such things.

In fact, I remember a realtor who drove us to a house via the scenic route. He no doubt thought we were so new to the area that we wouldn't realize he had gone miles out of the way to avoid some eyesores just around the corner from the house. Because of our prehousehunting scouting trip, we were wise to him. Be wary and be aware. You are the one who has to live in (and perhaps try to resell) the house. A drive around will also help you to realize just how far a particular house is from schools, stores, libraries, and whatever else may be important to you.

In order to assure yourselves time to do this driving around and checking, be sure, when planning your major househunting trip, to allow a day to yourselves—without the help (or hindrance) of a realtor. This will also give you a chance to check into any "by owners" you may have noticed in the paper or in your drives with the realtors.

In trying to arrive at a decision about a house, do not hesitate to see a particular house several times to be absolutely sure it's right for you. Shopping for a house isn't like shopping for a new dress or car, so be sure. No refunds!

It will help your decision making if you take copious notes about any and all houses you are even remotely considering. It can be very confusing at the end of a day of traipsing through dozens of houses to try to remember some of the houses you've seen, let alone remember small but important details. It is best to get listing sheets, which give such vital statistics as price, room dimensions, and type of heating system, from your realtor on any of the houses you like. These listing sheets are helpful as references and memory-joggers when you are trying to decide which house to buy.

You will want to make even more specific notes on the house you do finally choose (colors of all the rooms, carpets, and fixtures; window sizes if you need to buy curtains, etc.). It is amazing how much you can forget when you get away from a house, and it will be fun—and helpful in making plans—to have this information at your fingertips. And take some pictures for the folks back home.

Buying a Condominium

The purchase of a condominium (which is real estate that combines individual ownership of the inside space of a unit with joint, undivided, ownership of the outside) is a popular alternative to buying a single-family dwelling. (All the previous advice would still apply.) A condominium is particularly desirable, in fact usually the only option, if you wish to live in the downtown area and do not wish to rent.

Even if you are buying in the suburbs or in a small town, the purchase of a condo might be affordable when a single-family dwelling is not, since a condominium is usually cheaper than a single-family house with the same square footage in the same area. The reason for this is that even though you will own your own unit, you will be sharing undivided ownership of the space between units and the grounds with the other condo owners. In addition to sharing ownership, you share expense; so everyone saves! But make sure you *do* share this ownership and that it is not being held by the condo developer or anyone else. This common ownership should include the recreational facilities.

Another advantage to condo ownership is the freedom from maintenance chores while at the same time affording you the tax advantage of ownership and the investment of your money in real estate. Many people consider the purchase of a condominium the happy medium between renting an apartment and buying a single-family house.

Condominiums have homeowners associations, made up of all the unit owners, which hire a manager, set fees, decide on necessary repairs and improvements to common property, etc. Usually each unit gets one vote, though maintenance fees are usually assessed with respect to square footage, view, and location. The maintenance fee covers such items as management and operation costs. Since these fees vary from one condo to another, check carefully to make sure you are satisfied that they will be fair and affordable. Have an attorney review all papers before you sign, as there can be seemingly small differences between condominium developments that are, in legal reality, drastic differences. If you are tempted to buy a condominium for the first time, I recommend that you read *The Complete Condominium Guide* by Bruce Cassidy (New York: Dodd, Mead & Company, 1979) for more in-depth advice.

After Deciding . . . What Then?

Once you have decided on a house, relax. Don't keep asking yourself pointless questions such as, "Should we have bought a bigger one? A smaller one? None?!" I know that during the period between buying a house and moving in, I seem to dwell masochistically on the bad points of the house we have chosen. I even picture it smaller than it actually is. If you find yourself plagued by these same worries, it may comfort you to know that so far all the doubts and qualms as to whether or not we would really be satisfied with our new homes have disappeared once we have moved in and got settled.

After you relax and accept the fact that you *have* made a decision and *do* have a house, you can proceed to make sure that the closing on your new house goes smoothly. To help in this matter, you may want an attorney—for peace of mind, if nothing else, in such a major purchase. Try very hard to hire one recommended by a friend or coworker or attorney you trust in your present location. Do not ask your realtor or the present owner of the house to recommend one. That would be tempting fate, and you may never feel completely sure just whose interests were being protected.

The first thing you have to do, of course, when you decide on a house, is to reach an agreement with the seller. You will be at an advantage in negotiations if you have not oohed and aahed your way through the house in front of the present owner or the realtor. Do not appear *too* anxious. Let them think you just might be willing to pass up this house, and they just might be willing to accept the offer you make. Get out your poker face. Don't, however, carry this to the extreme of offending the property or its owner. It's hard to get a good bargain from someone who is angry with you.

Don't be afraid to make what the realtor may try to tell you is a ridiculously low offer. You can always come up, but you can't come down. Your offer can also consist of requests that they include certain items with the house, such as draperies, refrigerator, or storage shed. Chances are, you will receive a counteroffer from the seller, and you will end up settling for something between your offer and his initial asking price.

Many realtors recommend that an interested buyer make a 10 percent deposit when he makes an offer on a house.

Many buyers make a token $500 or $1,000 deposit with their purchase offer, which may contain a clause stating that the deposit will be increased once the seller accepts the offer and all contingencies, such as obtaining a mortgage loan, are removed. And, by the way, a contingency stating that a buyer is not bound to the agreement if he is unable to obtain financing is not an unreasonable or unusual contingency. On the contrary.

Never make your earnest-money check payable directly to the seller but rather to a neutral third party, such as the realtor, an attorney, an escrow firm, or a title company. Some sellers have been known to spend the earnest money before closing and were subsequently unable to refund it when the buyer became entitled to it. And you can't get blood from a turnip!

Mortgage Financing

Next you will need to obtain financing, and there are many ways to finance a home. The most common way is with a mortgage, which is a loan that uses the house as collateral and which is paid back in equal monthly payments over the next twenty-five or thirty years, with interest, of course, on the unpaid balance. Even though the total amount of the monthly payment never changes, the principal portion will increase and the interest portion will decrease each month.

Assuming an Existing Mortgage

You may be able to assume the remaining mortgage of the present owner, which will make closing costs considerably less because there will be less paperwork required. The interest rate on the old mortgage may be much lower than current rates too, or there may be a stipulation that you have to pay the going rate. One drawback is that assuming a mortgage frequently requires an enormous down payment because you have to cover the seller's equity (the sales price minus his existing mortgage). One way to circumvent this problem is with a second mortgage, which I will talk about later in this chapter.

I should point out, though, that whenever a house has an attractive assumable mortgage or the seller is willing to help you with financing, you cannot expect the price of the house to be lowered as much in negotiations as it might be otherwise, if indeed it is lowered at all.

FHA and VA Loans

You can check into mortgages that are insured by the Federal Housing Administration (FHA) or, if you are eligible, by the Veterans' Administration (VA). It should be stressed that these loans are made by banks, savings and loan associations, and other approved lenders and are *insured* by the government. They usually require a smaller down payment (sometimes *no* down payment with a VA loan) and often a lower monthly payment because the lender is protected from loss if you don't pay. (In the case of a VA loan, loss to the lender is insured to 60 percent of the appraisal value.)

FHA and VA loans are given only on property that has passed a stringent appraisal, thus affording you great peace of mind if you obtain one. They have their drawbacks, though. In days of high interest rates that exceed the interest ceiling set for these loans, it may be nearly impossible to get one. There is also considerable paperwork involved, so if time is of the essence this may not be the financial way to go. Also, the seller is required to pay the points, and this can be an obstacle (though usually not an insurmountable one) to one or both parties involved.

Conventional Loans

You may choose conventional financing from a savings and loan association, a commercial bank, a mortgage banker, a savings bank or an insurance company. You make a down payment of 10 to 25 percent of the property's cost and receive a mortgage loan for the remainder. Guidelines vary from one lending institution to another and from one part of the country to another, and certainly from one money market to another, but a common rule of thumb used by lending institutions is to loan two or two and one-half times your salary (and this should include *both* spouses' salaries). Others want your monthly loan payment to be no more than 25 percent of your monthly gross income(s) or total monthly obligations (house and car payments, phone bill, and other monthly obligations) to be no more than one-third of your gross income(s). Again, let me stress that these restrictions can vary from one place to another, so if you get turned down by one lending institution and truly feel you *can* afford the property, try another—try them all! For one thing, some of them will take into consideration commissions, bonuses, and benefits like company cars, and some won't. Needless to say, such items *can* make a big difference, but only if the lending institution will let them.

The Mortgage Contract

It can take several weeks before you hear whether or not your loan is approved, but your interview at the time of application should give you a fair idea of your chances. They will tell you right then and there if they think it is hopeless.

Be sure to shop around for a mortgage because interest rates and loan-origination fees and other important factors do vary. Before shopping for a mortgage, prepare a list of questions to ask each lending agency, and prepare a comparison chart on which to record the answers you get. The information you will need will include the lender's name, the name and telephone number of the loan officer, the maximum loan amount or the percentage of the home's purchase price, variable or fixed interest rates (fixed are usually the best), maximum loan terms (twenty-five to thirty years is normal), monthly payment for principal and interest, any penalty for early repayment, any possibility of refinancing at a later date without charge, whether the mortgage can be assumed by a subsequent buyer and at what interest rate, whether you must escrow money for tax and insurance (with FHA and VA, you must), and closing costs (which include the title search, transfer taxes, insurance, and loan-origination fees).

Typical closing costs might include a loan-origination fee of two points (2 percent of the mortgage, or $1,200 on a $60,000 mortgage), a required appraisal by the lending institution for $75, title insurance for $75, recording fees of $3 for the deed and $7 for the mortgage, and a survey fee of $50, for a total of $1,410 in closing costs to be paid by the buyer. You will probably also have to pay the following year's premium for fire and hazard insurance on the house.

There are two clauses in particular you should look for when obtaining a mortgage. One is the *prepayment clause*, which stipulates that you can pay off all or part of your loan ahead of schedule without a penalty. Some conventional mortgages do not allow you to do this because, of course, they would lose interest money. The other one is the *open-end clause*, which enables the borrower to refinance his loan without paying additional finance charges.

A weekly profile of mortgage terms and availability is published in many areas by local title-insurance companies or the local board of realtors. Your mortgage shopping would be greatly facilitated if you could obtain one. Remember that timing is important in getting the best mortgage terms. Many lenders set their quotas at the beginning of each month, so, especially in days of tight money, it is best to have your loan application ready before the first of the month.

The Second Mortgage

Sometimes a buyer needs a second mortgage to enable him to purchase a property if he cannot come up with enough down payment. A second mortgage is frequently carried by a seller or a builder who does not have to have all his equity at once. There are three types of second mortgages that we should discuss.

An *amortizing second mortgage* works like a regular mortgage, with equal payments, the interest portion decreasing and the principal portion increasing each month. But on the second mortgage, the repayment is done in a much shorter period of time, perhaps five years.

Another type of second mortgage is the *graduated mortgage* payment, which consists of gradually increasing payments from start to finish.

The third type of second mortgage is the *balloon mortgage.* Here monthly payments are relatively small—usually about half of what they would be under an amortized mortgage and sometimes covering only the interest—with the portion of the loan that is still unpaid (perhaps as much as two-thirds of the loan) being paid in one lump sum at the end of the loan period.

Contract for Deed

Another financing alternative to consider, as either a buyer or a seller of property, especially when money is tight or interest rates high, is a *contract for deed*, also called a *land contract*. This method enables the seller to earn interest income, but it also keeps him from realizing the future appreciation on the property. A contract for deed is a written agreement by which the buyer agrees to pay the seller in installments the established price plus interest over a certain number of years, with the title remaining with the seller until the purchase price or some specified portion of it (frequently 50 percent) is paid. If the buyer defaults, he forfeits the payments already made.

This type of financing can be done in any of the three ways mentioned for second mortgages, or in any other way that is agreeable to the two parties involved. It can be short-term or long-term, and it can be for part of the loan needed by the buyer or all of it. Sometimes similar arrangements are made under a lease with option to buy, whereby all or part of the rent paid will be applied toward the purchase price of the home if the tenant decides to buy at a specified price within a certain period of time.

Getting Mortgage Financing

We hear a lot about creative financing today, and certainly here is where an intelligent and informed—and creative—realtor can help you consummate a purchase *or* a sale by checking out all possible financial arrangements. And have your attorney make sure it is not just creative financing you are getting, but legal and fair too.

When you go to apply for a loan, it will greatly expedite matters if you take with you credit references, bank account numbers and balances, proof of your present mortgage balance, and appraisals on the home you are trying to sell. Also, take a list of assets (stocks, bonds, cars—anything that can improve your financial picture) and debts.

When you close on your new house, be sure that everything that was agreed to in the earnest-money contract has been carried out. If something has not been done (maybe the new driveway has not yet been poured as promised), then you must set aside the appropriate amount of money in an escrow account, whereby the seller would not be paid for such items until they are completed as agreed.

If it is at all possible, however, avoid the escrow business entirely by buying something already completed to your satisfaction or by planning to take care of it yourself or by refusing to close until everything is completed. We learned from experience (our great but often painful teacher) that whereas an escrow account does insure that the seller will not get his money until an agreement has been fulfilled, there are too many ways he can get around it for an extension of time. In the meantime, *you* don't have the money, either—or the item that you have, in effect, paid for.

At the time of closing, if not before, have the people from whom you are buying give you the warranties and service manuals for the furnace and appliances. You might also want to ask for names of competent service people.

Building a Home

Some of you may have the time and courage to build a new home. Almost as important as choosing the right house and right building site is choosing the right contractor. Before deciding whether to hire a particular contractor, find out how long he's been in business, whether he has a fixed address, and whether he does the work himself or sub-contracts it. By all means, try to see some of the homes he has built. Check on his reputation, reliability, and workmanship by asking local building-materials suppliers, bankers, the better business bureau, and others for whom and with whom he has worked. Find out if the contractor gives a warranty on his work. For how long? Will it cover materials and labor?

You should get at least three bids. The cheapest bid may not necessarily be the most satisfactory. Other factors may be more important, such as reputation and the services promised in the contract. Be sure you have a written contract. The more detailed and specific the contract as to grade of materials and quality of workmanship, the better protected you will be.

If you choose to engage the services of an architect instead of using one of the builder's house plans, you will want to use the same care you have used in choosing the other professionals involved in your move. Ask for recommendations and references.

If you are building, you may wish to do some of the work yourself—if you have the time, talent, or training. (If you don't have the training, maybe you have the time to acquire some through one of the many available courses at a local college, vocational school, or adult education program.) Doing some of the work yourself, whether it is something "little" like the wallpapering and painting, or something major like acting as your own contractor, subcontracting the various jobs (electrical, plumbing, sheetrocking, etc.), can save you money. It will also cost you time, so decide which you have more of—time or money.

Or perhaps you will want to build the house by your own labor (a favorite dream of my husband's, which thus far I have thankfully succeeded in delaying if not entirely squelching). If so, you will have to be prepared for the financial difficulties you are likely to face from incredulous bankers. After all, the house is their collateral, and they may have doubts as to the worth of a house you have constructed with your own two (amateur) hands.

Renting

You may want to rent rather than buy, especially if you are moving to a new location and want time to get to know your surroundings well enough to choose where you want to live on a more permanent basis. Or, perhaps you want to rent while you build or save for a house or condominium. If you don't mind moving twice, this can be advantageous. Or perhaps you just want to rent! Renting can free you from much responsibility, such as upkeep and the worry about resale if you plan to move again.

If you are going to be renting, take careful note of a few things before you sign a lease. As a tenant, you have the right to know who the landlord is. This will be important if legal action should ever be taken. Don't settle for the name of the manager.

You should know the amount of rent and when it is due, the amount of the security deposit and the conditions for its return, what utilities are paid for by the landlord and what utilities are paid for by you. Find out whether pets and/or children are allowed. Ask how much notice must be given if you want to move out when the lease expires and also the conditions for subletting. Your new lease should include a transfer clause if you have the slightest chance of needing it. The conditions under which you can make alterations should be in writing, as well as who is responsible for making repairs and keeping common hallways clean. In fact, get *everything* in writing!

Security deposits are a common area of dispute, so ask for a written statement explaining what must be done to get the deposit back when your lease expires. Also agree in writing as to the condition when you moved in. Get written acknowledgment of any damage, no matter how slight, found on your initial inspection. Be wary of promises made by landlords unless they are in writing. Otherwise, you may wait forever for that dripping faucet to be fixed.

If you are renting an apartment, you will want to find out what type of security system they have, if any, and what recreational facilities are available and whether or not there is an additional fee for them. Look over the pool, tennis courts, and whatever else there is very carefully to make sure they are being properly maintained. After all, you will be paying for them—if not in a separate fee, then with each monthly rent check. Find out what laundry facilities are available and whether they will be adequate for your needs. Same with parking.

In order to evaluate an apartment accurately, sometimes (indeed, all the time) it is wise to talk to one of the tenants. With a little ingenuity, you should be able to swing that. A tenant can point out, even if the manager won't, that you'll be able to hear your neighbor's toilet flush. Or, if you're lucky, a tenant may honestly assure you that you've found a great place to live.

You've come a long way in your move now. You've organized the entire move on paper, you've disposed of a home, and you've acquired a new one in which you can live happily ever after (or at least until the next move). But, alas, some of your busiest moments are yet to come. So stop, take another deep breath, and let's get into the heart of this move.

CHECKLIST

As Soon as You Learn of a Move

Make lists of what you want in an area and house.

Begin search, via realtors' listing sheets and newspapers, for new home.

Get all available information from chamber of commerce.

If possible, visit new location and decide on area(s) in which you would like to live.

At Least Six Weeks Prior to Move

Begin househunting in earnest.

Decide on a house.

Make offer.

Engage services of attorney.

If buying, sign purchase agreement. If renting, sign lease.

Apply for financing, if necessary.

Open checking and savings accounts in new locale.

At Closing

Take certified or cashier's check in amount your attorney or the lending institution has indicated.

Insure new home.

Obtain keys, garage-door-opener devices, service manuals for appliances and furnace, etc., from previous owner.

5

MOVING ON

Since you now have a new home and address, it is not too soon to start the changes of address. You can get an address-change kit at your post office—free! First-class mail will be forwarded free, but all second-class magazines and newspapers and third-class mail of value are forwarded postage due, and then only if you request and promise to pay such postage due, for ninety days. The same is true of parcels. If you refuse this postage-due mail, the postmaster at the forwarding office will discontinue forwarding any more of that class mail. You can simplify matters and save money by getting your kit and using it early.

If you start soon enough, you can include many address changes when you are paying monthly bills on credit cards, utilities, department stores, etc. This saves an extra effort as well as extra stamps. Magazines should be notified as soon as possible; they usually take at least eight weeks to process. You will expedite matters if you include an address label from a recent issue.

If you are moving out of town, I suggest you reserve notifying distant friends and relatives who may not already know of your move until after you are settled in your new home. There is usually more of a need for communication with old friends then. For now, spare time (if you can find any) is probably better spent with dear ones that you will soon be leaving.

About a month before you move to a new area, it is wise to stop writing checks on your account in your present location. This will allow time for all checks to clear, and you can close your account before moving.

Moving Companies

If you are hiring professional movers to pack and move you, as we were fortunately able to do, your work load will be greatly minimized. You will have the best luck scheduling the move to fit your needs if you make arrangements with a moving company as early as possible. We have always notified them five weeks in advance of moving day, which is none too soon.

We have used two different moving companies, both nationally known, and for all practical purposes they provided identical services. Most major nationwide movers have the same rate per one hundred pounds. Rates are governed by the carrier's tariff, which is filed with the government. Still, I would shop around to compare service, and you may wish to check out smaller companies.

After you have contacted a company, they will send a representative out to make a premove inspection and estimate the cost of your move. You must have someone present who knows which items will go and which will stay. Discuss with your mover the protection for your possessions being moved. The carrier's liability, unless specifically increased by you, is limited to only sixty cents per pound, which is probably inadequate for most of the articles being moved. Be sure that agreements between you and the carrier are in writing and on the order for service and the bill of lading.

When planning your moving dates, remember that you get better service if you don't move at the end of the month and if you don't move during the summer. Don't be afraid to insist on definite dates for packing, loading, and—this will be the hardest, but remind them that you are paying plenty and you have plenty of rights—delivery. We have had movers try to delay delivery a day or two past what we felt was a reasonable date. We refused to accept this, since it would have meant an expensive stay in motels. Even worse, it would have meant being cooped up with the kids in a motel when we were anxious to get settled in our new home. On the other hand, the movers might want to rush you. Just because they may be capable of driving all night after loading your belongings does not mean you are. Be reasonable, but assertive. We have found them most cooperative.

You will need to let the van line know your new address, as well as specific directions. They will also want a number where they can reach you en route or at destination or, preferably, both.

Carriers are not permitted to transport pets, houseplants, perishable food, articles likely to cause spills or fires, or articles of intangible value. We moved our plants ourselves, packing them carefully in our camper and station wagon. We were highly successful despite the chilly November drafts.

Our frozen foods we handled by eating before we left. As luck would have it, I had frozen our first good crop of strawberries as well as crate after luscious crate of peaches shortly before we learned of one transfer. We had looked forward to enjoying these fruits of my labor over the long winter but instead found ourselves eating them every night during the last weeks before we moved. I haven't bothered to freeze either strawberries or peaches since, for the simple reason that no one in this family any longer has an appetite for them. We also tried to eat as many of our canned goods and staples as we could. It made that much less to unpack and put away in our new home, not to mention reducing our shipping weight and cost.

In addition to our plants, we also kept with us our stocks and bonds from our safe deposit box. But be sure *you* put them in a safe place for transport and get them into a new safe deposit box before they get misplaced. You may prefer to send your birth certificates, stocks, etc., by registered mail to your new address.

Do not plan to move flammables or aerosol cans with you for the same reason that the moving company won't take them. It's dangerous! Give them away or throw them away.

Even if you do contract with a moving company, you may still want to pack and personally move any really sentimental or monetary valuables to insure that they arrive and arrive safely. On the other hand, if you are like us, you will have more faith in the movers accomplishing this, since they won't have three rambunctious kids and a playful pup sandwiched between plants and suitcases.

You can protect yourselves by making a photographic record of silverware, expensive crystal or china, and other valuables. Place small objects on a table or flat, plain-colored rug, and take a close-up picture. Snapshots of antique or ornate furniture will help if repair work becomes necessary. Such pictures can also back up claims for damages incurred during a move.

Packing and Moving Yourself

We have made only the smallest of moves without professional help, so I talked with others who are more qualified to advise you as to how you would best go about packing and moving yourself.

Bruce, who is an old hand at this type of move, said "Start early to collect sturdy boxes and then carefully pack as much as you can as soon as you can."

I elicited a few trade secrets from a professional packer, which I will share in case you are going to do some or all of your packing. "Do keep in mind, though, that the van line is not responsible for damage to items packed by you," Clayton reminds us.

For chinaware and glassware, put two or three inches of cushioning material in the bottom and then pack the heaviest and largest pieces first. Wrap each piece separately with at least two thicknesses of paper. Start by placing wrapped pieces at the outside edge of the container and fill in toward the center. Insert a layer of dishes, then a layer of cushioning, up to within two to three inches from the top; then fill with more cushioning material (maybe some of your dish towels? less to pack elsewhere!). Stemware should be placed upright for greater protection. Don't let the container get too heavy.

The best protection for the bindings of books is to wrap each book in two thicknesses of paper and place on end in a small carton. Again, do not let the box get too heavy. Phonograph records should be in their albums and wrapped and placed in a container so that they stand on edge.

Framed pictures should be protected by crisscross strips of masking tape to reinforce the glass. Do not extend the strips over the frames as they can leave a residue of adhesive. Lamp shades should be wrapped separately in clean white tissue (not newspaper—it may smudge them). Do not force one shade inside another.

Defrost and thoroughly dry the inside of your refrigerator and freezer. Let them air for twenty-four hours before the move. (Do this even if you aren't packing or moving yourself.) Wrap paper around each shelf and allow it to hang out over the edge facing the door to prevent scratching and chipping. In some cases, especially with older models, the power unit must be securely tied down to prevent damage.

Small clocks should be well wrapped and packed either with bedding or somewhere where they can't slide. Grandfather clocks will need special servicing. Small electric kitchen appliances should be wrapped with paper and padding to prevent scratching and then placed in the bottom of containers. Kitchenware should be wrapped in double thicknesses of newspaper and packed in sturdy containers with the heavier items in the bottom.

Put a fitted sheet on each mattress, and under this sheet place a top sheet and a lightweight blanket. You will be all set to make your bed quickly and hop in the first night in your new home. The rest of the bedding and linens can be packed in large cartons or used to fill chests and dresser drawers or used as cushioning. Do not overload funiture drawers or shelves; excess weight causes damage. It is nice to use specially constructed clothing wardrobes for moving clothing from the closets—lessens the need for ironing. Pack only enough clothing in each carton to fit snugly without wrinkling.

Secure all caps of medicines and toilet articles. If you're going far, seal these with a coat of clear nail polish around the edge of each cap where it touches the top of bottles or with a strip of cellophane tape over each cap. Pack firmly with paper or wash cloths between bottles, with the bottles upright. Mark the container *Fragile* and *This End Up*.

Pack hand tools in containers, limiting the weight to fifty to sixty pounds. Disassemble power tools as much as possible and pack parts separately. Long-handled tools, such as shovels and rakes, should be tied together. Mark all containers as to their contents and the rooms you want them placed in on arrival.

Of course, if you are just moving a few blocks away, you will not need to take such great care with most things. You will also probably be able to move boxes of your belongings a little at a time, perhaps even getting things unpacked and put away before bringing the next load over. You might need a truck and helpers only when it is time to move the furniture.

If I were going to move myself, I would have a *moving party* to which I would invite friends to help in return for a little beer (a *little* until after the work was accomplished, anyway) and a lot of camaraderie. We have helped friends who were moving themselves and have not minded in the least. If you are moving a great distance, however, you would have to also have an unloading party on a different day with different people. Maybe a van line would be cheaper, after all?

Stopping and Starting Services

Sometime during the last few weeks before your move, you can make arrangements to have your present telephone service stopped. I always ask that they disconnect our service late in the last day that we will be in the house. This is the day that we are cleaning up after the movers leave, and I usually find it necessary (or at least desirable) to use the phone then. After all, there are many people that I will soon have to *pay* to call. The phone company can stop service without coming to the house, and you can let them know where they can find a key to come for the equipment at a later date.

While you're in the phone business, it is a good time to call collect the phone company in your new area to arrange to have service started the day you will be arriving. This is important. Have the service started the day (if not the *minute*) you arrive. You will see in a later chapter that there are numerous things to get organized, many of which can be handled more quickly over the phone.

Call your doctors and dentists a few weeks before you move to see if they can recommend replacements in your new city. Otherwise you can rely on the AMA or a neighbor in your new area, but it is sometimes more comforting to have a professional suggest someone he feels will be competent to take care of you and yours. Also arrange to have your records sent to your new doctors and dentists, but please not before the date of your move! You may need them here yet. You can, however, make these and many other such requests early. Just be sure to let them know the date the request is *effective* (the date of Moving Day).

Talk to your insurance agent to see about changing or ending coverage here. Arrange for discontinuing milk service, water-softener service, etc. Arrange to have your utilities stopped and check on all possible refunds from gas, electricity, water, or oil company (if you have sold your home). Just phone—companies will send your check and do not usually require your initial deposit receipt. Be sure you have your homeowner's insurance started on your new house, and notify your car insurance agent if you're moving far, since rates vary from one location to another.

More Lists

When you have just one or two weeks before Moving Day, you should make some more lists. Before the *real* rush (yes, you ain't seen nothin' yet!) and while you can still think clearly, make lists of things you do not want to be packed or moved.

The first list should contain the *Things to be Left in House*

for New Owners—garage-door-opener devices, instructions
for all the appliances, keys to such things as the compactor
or the gas-fireplace starter, the list to help the new owners
become adjusted to their new home and area, and a phone
book (take one phone book with you for addresses).

You will also want a list of *Things to Keep with Us, Not
the Movers, during the Move.* It will include such items as
cleaning materials (vacuum cleaner, rags, cleaning agents,
mop, toilet brush, and anything else you need to clean the
house after the movers leave and perhaps to use in the new
house before the arrival of your furniture). This list should
also denote what you want to take in your car with you in
suitcases, boxes, or whatever. You will want to have clothes
and personal items, enough not only to get you through the
day the movers arrive (supposedly) at your new location but
also for an extra day or two to allow time for you to uncover
everything that has been boxed.

You may also want to have a box containing coffee pot,
coffee, and any other essentials you will want before you get
to the unpacking. If you have infants or toddlers, be sure to
keep their favorite sleeping companion with you rather than
with the movers. Also, any familiar daytime "friends"
would be nice for them to have as soon as they arrive in their
new home. This list may include plants and a cooler of any
frozen goods you have not been able to consume. Also include on this list, lest you forget, any valuables you plan to
keep with you.

Preparing for the Packers

A few days before Moving Day, clear out one closet where
you can put the things you have on these lists. Put a note on

the outside of this closet door telling the packers and movers, "Everything in this closet STAYS". You may even find it necessary to designate two closets for this purpose.

A day or two before the packers are to arrive, remove all pictures and other wall hangings that are to be moved. The packers will pack them, but they prefer not to be responsible for deciding which ones go and which ones stay or for any damage that may result from removing them from the walls. This will give you time to patch and paint any holes you may have left after removing pictures and nails. This is absolutely mandatory if you haven't sold the house yet and only common courtesy if you have. Unplug the television twenty-four hours prior to Moving Day to prevent damage.

The packers will come one or two days before the movers, depending on how much you have to be packed and how many workers they assign to you. There are two schools of thought as to whether or not you should stay around when the packers are there. My journal contains my philosophy regarding this.

10/29/75

    The packers came this morning. I decided to trust them with all our valuables (hee hee) since they are bonded employees. I can't help but feel that I would only be in their way and they in mine; plus, I'd much rather spend my last hours with Mom, not the packers! I was here to let them in and show them the pot of coffee I had made for them (maybe they'll take a little greater care with our things?). Before I left, though, I made sure all the waste baskets were emptied, as I have heard stories from other movees about the full ash trays and other ridiculous things being packed and moved right along with the good china. I guess it isn't part of the movers' jobs to make such a decision!

My neighbor Karen gasped in amazement when she learned I was actually going to leave the packers alone in our house. "For one thing," she said, "most employees do work faster when being watched by their employer." I had to agree with that. I always felt, however, that time—time to be with my friends and family here—was running out on me, so I spent this day or two visiting with them. Perhaps a happy medium would be to visit someone close to the house so you could pop in and out!

At any rate, whatever you do during the packing days, you will probably want to spend the nights with friends or family in town, since the house will be a maze of boxes by the end of a packing day. You will, of course, want to be at your house in the morning to let the packers in and at the end of the day to check on things and lock the house. And give the packers a phone number where they can reach you if they have questions or problems.

D-Day

Moving Day. Yes, it does finally arrive. After all the weeks of saying the words and planning for it, but not really believing it will ever come, it has a way of coming all too soon! But it is exciting, isn't it?

You will be given a personal inventory of household goods and personal property by your carrier. Keep it for a reference. You may need it to collect any damage or loss claims. You should make sure that a proper description of the condition of your furniture is entered on the inventory. Before signing the inventory, note on it by item number any exceptions you may have. Be certain that everything listed on the inventory is accounted for before the van operator leaves either at origin or destination. I have just given you some very good advice, but quite frankly, if your possessions are as numerous as ours, you may not be able to follow it completely. Do the best you can!

If you can, accompany your carrier to the weighing station for the weighing of your shipment. Ask for a final cost so that you can have the needed cash, money order, or certified check ready at destination.

I have always tried, and never succeeded, cleaning around the movers in my haste to get back with family and friends. However, the movers have a way (and I am sure it is quite necessary in the efficient loading of their van) of taking a few items from each room, when what I hope for is that they will completely empty one room (so that I can be cleaning it) before they proceed to the next. Usually all I can do while they are still there is scour sinks and bathtubs and toilets, wash out cupboards and closet shelves, polish woodwork, and wash windows. Did I say *all*? When the movers do leave, you can finish. With no furniture to dust or get in the way, you can whip through with a vacuum and mop quite quickly.

If you haven't sold your house yet, and if 'tis the season, you'd better winterize it. Also, notify the police if it is going to be vacant. Then wrap up your final bag of garbage. I'm sure one of your neighbors would just love to keep it for you until the next garbage pick-up day. Well, I'm sure you can find one neighbor who would at least be *willing* to keep it.

Empty the closets of the things you set aside to keep with you. Now make a thorough check of rooms, closets, attic, and garage for items the movers may have overlooked. Then shut the windows, set the thermostat, lock the doors, and bid farewell to a house you will undoubtedly always feel nostalgic about. At least *I* have a way of growing extremely fond of each and every abode. I even dream about them with the same longing that I do dear old friends. I suppose it's the memories that each home holds for me.

Back to practical matters. Now you can drop the keys off at the realtor's or, if you were lucky enough to have sold the house yourself, deliver them to the new owners. It will probably be the end of a very long day by now, so you'd better get a good night's sleep to fortify yourself for the tearful good-byes and trip to the new home tomorrow.

You will want to plan to arrive at your new home as soon as possible. You need to be there when your household goods arrive. The carrier will charge an additional rate for excess waiting time, and goods placed in storage are subject to a thirty-day minimum charge. Contact the van line upon your arrival in the new location so they know where to reach you.

Drive safely!

CHECKLIST

As Soon as Possible

Complete changes of address.
Notify van line.
If you are going to pack yourself, start collecting and saving sturdy boxes and newspapers.
Begin decreasing inventory of frozen foods, groceries, and other items.

Thirty Days before Move

If you are moving out-of-town, stop writing checks on old account.
If you are packing yourself, start packing!

Three Weeks before Move

Have all records (medical, dental, school, church, etc.) transferred or obtain them to take yourself.
Make arrangements for insurance coverage changes.
Make travel plans and get necessary motel reservations.

Two Weeks before Move

Arrange to have services here stopped (milk, cleaners, water softener, phone, garbage, newspaper, and, if house is sold, water and utilities).

Arrange to have new services started (utilities, water, phone, newspaper and garbage).

Make arrangements to have appliances serviced for move.

Return borrowed items.

The Week before Move

Dispose of flammables.

Pack suitcases.

Close bank accounts and transfer funds.

Organize things to keep with you during move to new house.

Remove pictures and hangings from wall and touch up paint as necessary.

Clear out one closet to put items to be left behind or to go with you, not the movers.

The Day before Move

Clean and air refrigerator and freezer.

Unplug television.

Clean and air range.

Finish personal packing.

Moving Day

Clean house.

Accompany movers to weigh station and obtain final cost.

Get payment ready to give movers at destination.

Dispose of garbage.

Check all closets and cupboards.

Winterize home, if necessary.
Set thermostat.
Shut off faucets.
Turn off lights.
Shut and lock all windows and doors.
Leave keys.

Upon Arrival at New House
Notify van line of your arrival.
Clean house.

6

HOME (?!) AT LAST

I've heard horror stories about people's household shipments being a week or two late or lost or—well, let's not ask for trouble. Let's be reassured by the knowledge that our family's three shipments were delivered as promised.

Initial Unpacking

As the movers are delivering and unloading, you will want to be sure they are putting the boxes in the proper rooms. It will make your unpacking go so much faster, not to mention easier, since you won't have to lug around boxes that weigh more than you do.

No doubt you will have decided earlier whether you are going to unpack the boxes yourselves or have the moving company unpack them. Even if you aren't concerned about saving money, I would advise you to unpack yourself. The one and only time we were going to hire the unpacking done, we learned we would have to wait until two days after the delivery for the unpackers to come. Forget that! Two days after the delivery, I had us almost totally unpacked.

Even if they could unpack you immediately, I don't believe it is the best way. I have been told that the unpackers do just that—unpack. They don't decide, nor would you want them to, where the cinnamon should go or which side of the closet your husband should have. I really feel you would be wise to unpack yourself and put things away as you go along. Can you imagine a house with all your belongings sitting around wherever the packers were able to find a spot to set them?

On the other hand, if you are pressed for time and just want things out of the way for now, it would save countless hours of unwrapping each and every item you possess (from your globe to your measuring spoons). You could just toss things in closets and cupboards as the unpackers unpack them and then organize them later at your convenience. My husband wants to try it that way next time. He didn't think he'd *ever* get the last of his workbench paraphernalia unpacked last time. (Come to think of it, I'm not sure he *has*.)

I always start my unpacking as soon as the movers start unloading. I get in a central location (usually the kitchen) and am able to direct them with furniture placement while I empty boxes. Any boxes you are able to empty while the movers are still there can be removed from the premises by them. The value of that is not to be underestimated, since all other boxes will probably have to be broken down by you if you want your garbage service to take them away. (I always break the boxes down as I go along. Experience has taught me that there is nothing worse than breaking down one hundred boxes at one crack.)

Depending on the ages of your children, unpacking can be a fun thing for them to do and a big help to you. I cringed at the thought of my kids going through the boxes when we moved the last time. It was summer, and they were looking for something to do, so I reluctantly gave in to their pleas to let them unpack the boxes for their bedrooms. Kerri, who was ten, had her room looking absolutely perfect (quite unlike its appearance at this very moment) in no time. She hung up all her clothes, made the beds, organized books, and soon had the "best room in the house."

The other, younger, kids weren't able to accomplish quite that much, but they did unwrap countless of their valuables such as Barbie dolls, marbles, and posters of John Travolta. When Kerri finished her room, she went on to help them with the harder chores of room organizing and then helped me unpack and put away linens and bathroom supplies, etc. She thought it was fun, and it saved me time and energy. While the movers are still there, however, it is important to stay out of their way, so the kids are better *out*side on this day. They can start helping tomorrow!

Before the movers leave, be sure they have done all they agreed to do (e.g., set up beds, reassemble sewing machine). They should put back together anything they took apart for the move.

The movers will need your signature again before they leave. If you do not agree with something on the inventory sheet regarding the condition or loss of something, mark the sheet accordingly before signing it. You should file claims immediately, but you may not discover the damage or loss until you become more settled. Remember that you do have nine months from the date of delivery to make a claim. You must have proof of your claim. The best proof will be the written notations you made at the time of delivery on the shipping papers. Also, save any broken or damaged items, even if they do look more like garbage than evidence.

The Move-In Process

Once the movers leave, you can really dig in. It has always taken me just one week for what I call the Move-in Process, which takes me to the point where we are comfortably set-

tled (i.e., no boxes around). It may take you more or less time
than that, depending on your individual circumstances and
preferences. For one thing, I have had no babies around
when I moved. The kids were always school-age, which af-
forded me the time to work, work, work until the boxes were
all unpacked and disposed of and the last picture was hung.

I can never relax until I have reached this point. In fact, I
admit to a rather perverse enjoyment of all the work required
to organize a new home. It always pleases me to see things
begin to fall into place, and to see how different pieces of
furniture and accessories end up looking made to order in
completely different rooms and settings from the previous
house. Yes, that picture from the old bathroom just might
look downright elegant on the dining room wallpaper!

My friend Natalie shares my enjoyment of the Move-in
Process. She says, "The reason I enjoy it is that it not only
gives me a feeling of accomplishment, but it is so *noticeable*
to everyone, unlike routine housework that no one ever
seems to appreciate." Amen.

However, the fact that I am unable to relax until I have
completed the Move-in Process leads to a rather strained atmosphere around the new house. Therefore, it is good that it
takes me only a week. For those with my temperament, I
would recommend that you not draw it out any longer than
necessary. Others of you may be the type who would benefit
from a break to read a good book or knit a few stitches or go
out on the town. Do whatever you need to do to survive this
period.

Here are a couple of journal entries from the end of my
Move-in Process.

11/5/75

Emptied the last of the boxes and hung the last picture
today. That brief entry makes it seem like today wasn't too

busy, eh, Diary? Well, I was so busy trying to reach the point where I could say that I "emptied the last box and hung the last picture" that I am too tired to write anything else tonight.

11/6/75

Oh, what fun to awake to a house that looks like a home! There are a few gaps, though, so after I got the kids off to school, I had a second cup of coffee and balanced the checkbook. After verifying that we did indeed have some money left, I went shopping. I bought a few hanging plants for the dining room, bedrooms, and one of the bathrooms. I bought some new towels to go with our new bathroom colors and also a few new wastebaskets. I also bought a couple of little knickknacks—kind of a housewarming present for myself. There's nothing like shopping and spending money to lift one's spirits!

Reassuring Your Children

Whether you take a week, a month, or a year (believe me, I have talked to some who sheepishly confess to a few still un-packed boxes after a year), there are other things that must be done besides the requirements of the house. First and foremost to me and probably to all of you with children, even if it means *never* completing the Move-in Process, is doing anything and everything necessary and possible to help the kids make a fast, easy adjustment. This is so impor-tant, in fact, that I will devote the entire next chapter to it.

Once you have your children on the road to a happy ad-justment, there are still many other things to do before you can relax and get out your *List of Things to Do When Moved and Bored.* Besides just (?!) getting the house in order, there are approximately 1 million other things that need your attention.

As always, consult your lists. You will see that you need to do such things as arrange any services that you were unable to do before the move, get new driver's license, get license plates for cars, join a church, join a library, and—well, you can see that if the first week or two kept you too busy with the housework to get lonely, the next couple of weeks will keep you too busy with errands such as these.

Listing Tax Deductions

Whether it is early in a tax year or soon approaching April 15, take time to get all tax items relating to the move organized while everything is still fresh in your mind. If you have done your own tax returns in the past, then don't let a move during the tax year scare you out of doing them again. On the other hand, if you have never enjoyed doing them yourself or never felt you had the time or ability, this would not be the year to start. Regardless, it is still up to you to keep careful records.

You should have kept careful track of all the articles you gave to charities in the process of cleaning out your old residence. You will need to attach to Form 1040, Schedule A, a statement that gives a description, date, and manner of valuation of all the donated items. If you or your spouse are changing employers or are transferred or are self-employed and if your change in job location has added at least thirty-five miles to the distance from your old residence to your work, most moving expenses are tax deductible up to a total of $3,000. Keep records of all moving costs. You will be able to deduct househunting trips before the move, temporary living expenses, fees incurred for buying, selling, or leasing a residence, and transportation expenses in moving household goods and personal effects even if you don't itemize deductions.

For moving expenses incurred in a job transfer, your employer must furnish you with a statement, usually on Form 4782, detailing moving expense payments to you if a reimbursement or payment of moving expenses was made. All reimbursed moving expenses are considered compensation for income tax purposes, but most of this can be offset by deductions as mentioned above. You will need to fill out and attach Form 3903 for moving expenses.

It is also important to remember that you can defer the tax on the gain from the sale of your principal residence if the purchase price of the new residence is equal to or greater than the adjusted sales price of the old residence. You will need to file Form 2119, and it will be necessary for you to have all receipts and records of improvements made on your home as well as expenses incurred in fixing it up for the sale. In order to defer the tax, you must purchase your new residence within eighteen months of the sale of your old residence; if you are building, construction must have begun within eighteen months and you must use it as your principal residence within twenty-four months. The IRS regulations change frequently, so get updated instructions and check with your local office if you have any questions or problems in filing your return.

The Lull

Once you have completed the house and the reorganization of your lives, you can probably use the therapy of some out-of-town company—someone you feel close to and miss. I don't think any of our friends or family has ever given us a more precious gift than a visit as soon as possible after one of our moves. Even though new neighbors and acquaintances have always been very cordial to us (and later become great friends of ours), there is nothing, after the first few weeks of the hard work of a Move-in, like an already familiar face—someone with whom you can let it all hang out. After working so hard, no one wants to sit and make small talk with a stranger; better to relax with a close friend. *Then* it is easier to dig into the challenge of establishing new relationships.

We have always had at least three sets of company starting a couple of weeks after a move. So, now we are looking at a minimum of six weeks busy prior to a move, two to four weeks busy with the move, and then a month or more busy with company. Who could possibly complain about a lull after all that? In fact, a lull is just what the doctor (probably a psychiatrist) ordered at this point, though a little lull goes a long way.

Each time we have moved, we have quite enjoyed our lull (usually of about two months duration). Granted, it contains its down moments. In fact, the journal I kept has quite a smattering of entries such as these.

11/4/75

Mom and Dad called tonight, and it is hard to express the gamut of emotions that poured over me. First of all, it was oh-so-delicious to hear their familiar voices, but when I remembered that they were coming from three hundred, not three, miles away, I felt incredibly sad. I managed to stay brave to make the most of our telephone time. (But I still thought of a lot I wanted to say *after* we hung up. Maybe I should start keeping notes to refer to when they call. Better yet, I think I will start writing them a weekly letter, based mainly on what is going on in the kids' lives. Maybe then I won't feel so guilty about robbing them of the chance to watch their grandchildren grow up. It would also be good therapy for me to "talk" to them on paper each week.)

I felt completely devastated when we hung up. It's really sinking in. I had a good (who am I kidding? *bad*) cry—

the first time I've cried since we got here. Guess I've just been too busy.

12/13/75

Why did we move? I just miss everyone and everything so much! Even bowling today, which I joined to help keep my mind off "them," made me homesick. I found myself looking down the seating area and half expecting to see one of the old gang from back "home". Instead, what I saw were a bunch of happy strangers. I wonder if I'll ever feel happy with them. I shouldn't say that. They were all so friendly to me and really made me feel quite welcome. It's just so hard to move.

Fortunately, these feelings were few, far between, and short-lived. On the whole, some of my fondest memories are of our lulls. Never in all our busy, hectic, sometimes frantic lives are we so close as a family. Even though we all make the effort to make new friends as quickly as possible, believing this to be important, it does take time. During this period of time, we are each others' best friends, and we develop a closeness—husband/wife, parent/child, and child/child—that carries over even after we begin to go our separate ways again. It was shortly after our first move that I discovered that I enjoyed shopping with Kerri as much as I ever had with any of my friends. She and I (now often joined by younger sister Melissa) still relish an afternoon out for lunch and shopping together.

This lull seems to be a particularly good time to start fulfilling another of our traditions—the one whereby we treat the time in each new place as an extended vacation, whether it ends up being for eight months or eight years. We make sure that we see all the sights and places and attractions that any tourist there would want to see. We are determined not to be like our former neighbor Paula, who complained, "I have lived all my life in Chicago and have never been to the museums. As a matter of fact, I haven't been downtown for ten years."

When we lived in Minnesota, we were avid Viking and Twin fans (still are), and we skied, snowmobiled, and ice fished our way through the frigid winters. When we moved to South Dakota, we camped our way across the beautiful and varied terrain of that state. Our short stay of only eight months in Chicago kept us really on the move, taking in the museums, Sears Tower, and amusement parks. You name it—we did it. We're just beginning to explore our new home of Indianapolis and love the anticipation of discovering a whole new region of things to see and do. Wherever you are, buy a guidebook or call the chamber of commerce for brochures, and see the sights!

Another project that has kept us happily busy and busily happy is looking up and getting reacquainted with any friends or relatives we might have living in the new area. Our first move found us in the area in which my father was born and raised. I thought this was such a coincidence that it must be an omen that we were meant to live there. When the next move found us again near relatives and old friends, it dawned on me that this is just indicative of our small and transient world of today.

I must admit that I was hesitant on one of our moves to call my old cheerleading buddy from high school. We hadn't been in touch for twelve years (I'm not quite sure how I even knew she was in the Chicago area). I called, and it was amazingly great to talk to her. Don't put off calling someone because you feel you both might have changed. You probably have, but you may like the new yous even better.

The lull is also a good time to catch up on anything you have been neglecting during the more hectic months you have just lived through . . . or maybe even something you have been neglecting for years. Perhaps you need to bring your photo albums or baby books up to date. Or maybe you have a mountain of mending awaiting your nimble fingers. And don't forget to look at your list of *Things to Do When Moved and Bored.*

I know there are many of you out there who do not yet have time to get bored—you have to get busy and find a job. One of the biggest casualties of a job transfer can be the spouse's loss of a job—frequently a hard-earned, much-loved job. It only adds insult to injury to realize that your spouse is being transferred to an awaiting job (probably a promotion!) while you must pound the pavement in search of a new one when you already had a perfectly good one "back home!" Let's hope that you have already discussed this and vented your feelings in the earlier stages of your move, and you are now accepting the fact that you *are* no longer gainfully employed and if you wish to become so, you'd better get going. One small consolation for you at this point in the move is that boredom is not likely to be one of your problems (unless, of course, you get a boring job).

Whether you work outside the home or not, you will probably want to take advantage of any lull time to catch up on your rest and sleep after all you have just been through.

Separating the Lull from the Blahs

For this same reason, though—this stark contrast between the busy days and the lull—I always find myself particularly vulnerable to a severe case of the blahs (bordering on blues, in fact). So far, I have found it best for me to let the lethargy and depression run their course of about a week, during which time I do a lot of reading and eating. I have decided that it is just a natural reaction to the whole relocation business for me to crash after everything that *has* to be done

is done. Luckily, before too long I seem to get sick and tired
of acting sick and tired.

1/13/76

I think (hope!) that today I hit rock bottom. I didn't
even get dressed. I just crawled back in bed after the kids
were off to school. I got out when they came home from
school and again when John got home from work—but
only for a few minutes. I pleaded some vague symptoms of
headache and general malaise, but they were only true
because I had spent the entire day in bed. John was most
sympathetic about my "illness" (wonder if he suspects it's
really mental, not physical).

1/14/76

I'm sorry to report that today brought more of the same.
I didn't get out of bed for more than a few minutes at a
time (maybe I really am sick?), and each time, as I saw the
dishes piled in the sink and the lint covering the carpet, I
just sank into a deeper despair and crawled back under the
covers and buried myself into the lives of the people in my
books—yes, at least I am getting caught up on my reading.

You know, when we were in the thick of the move, with
things so hectic I thought I might die from overwork, I
looked longingly toward this time when things would settle down and I could just sit down with a good book or do
whatever else I wanted without worrying that it would
slow down the schedule. Well, that time is here, but
somehow it is not turning out quite like I had envisioned.
Talk about feast or famine. Well, after one week of this, I
can see that it is not going to change if someone doesn't
change it. I have a feeling I am the someone that holds that
power.

1/15/76

Part I of my plan was instituted this morning. I exer-
cised to an old Dave Clark V album—did some sit-ups, toe
touches, waist-bends, etc. Then I put on my parka and

jogging shoes, put Minnie on the leash, and off we went for a jog here and a walk there for a grand total of an utterly exhausting ten blocks. Exhausting for me, anyway; Minnie seemed to be just getting started when I headed us for home.

I collapsed on the kitchen chair and had my second cup of coffee, and then instead of feeling exhausted, I felt rosy-cheeked and exhilarated. I put on some more records—this time BTO and Grand Funk to really get me going—and whipped through the housework in what seemed like no time, but actually was all day (remember, I didn't do *anything* last week!).

Today when the kids got home from school I was able to share in their enthusiasm about the day's activities. They were happy to see I wasn't "sick" anymore. Tonight I joined the family around the fireplace and munched on popcorn with them—a definite improvement over the past week's solitary confinement in my bedroom, hearing the then-irritating sound of my family's laughter drift up the stairs to fill me with guilt.

1/16/76

Oh, how I wanted to go back to the stay-in-bed routine. I had to pry my sluggish body out of bed this morning. I really felt it was a life-or-death choice and that I *had* to keep up the pattern I started yesterday. I was happy to find, after a couple of cups of coffee and a quiet time with you, old Diary, that I actually felt equal to the task when the kids came bounding into the kitchen for their breakfast, lunch money, and hurried kisses good-bye. Could it be I've licked the battle of the blues?

Some version of this, less severe each time, has happened to me with every move. In getting myself reprogrammed, I always include some exercise to make me *feel* better and to help shed the pounds gained during my slump. I also make myself some lists of whatever it is I feel I should be doing. I do not put nearly the pressure on myself that I did during the move, but I do need *some* pressure and motivation, and for me lists work wonders. I feel so good crossing things off.

Welcome Wagon, etc.

One thing you might want to take advantage of if you're in a new area is the Welcome Wagon. There are other similar programs too that call on you and give you various gifts and cards entitling the bearer (you!) to all kinds of goodies from local merchants. It is not only nice to receive these items; it also gives you the added treat of getting out of the house to fetch them. You are enticed into acquainting yourself with many of the merchants and services available, at the same time learning your way around town.

To facilitate this, get a local map (your realtor or the chamber of commerce or the Welcom Wagon can supply you with one) and use it to find your way around. The combination of verbal directions and planning your route on a map is perfect for getting yourself oriented quickly. And the sooner you get oriented to your new surroundings, the happier you will be.

The Welcome Wagon also has meetings for newcomers and sometimes bridge clubs and bowling leagues. You not only meet people through these, but *new* people like yourself so you have an immediate common bond and something to talk about.

It is important for us women to talk to other relocated wives and mothers to compare problems and triumphs. The knowledge that there are so many others in the same situation has always been a tremendous help to me in a move. This, along with the fact that my husband (as well as the "higher-ups," his boss assured me recently) appreciates what the wife and family must contend with in a transfer, is not to be underestimated as a morale booster in a relocation.

Without exception, every place we have lived seems to be permeated with other nomads like us—and not just at Welcome Wagon functions. In each area, I find myself with a group of friends that is a nice combination of natives and transplants. It makes for an interesting group and verifies my theory that people everywhere are the same—great. I had reached this conclusion before we had even made our first move.

10/18/75

Tonight we went to the neighborhood farewell party for us. Really had a fun time. I will miss them all. I get quite upset wondering whether our new neighbors could possibly be this nice. I am able to rely on others here for help, whether for babysitting exchanges or a cup of sugar or an attentive ear. But when I realize that these neighbors come from Minnesota, Texas, South Dakota, London and India, I decide people must be basically the same everywhere, right?

Getting Involved

It is important to become involved in your new location, whether it is through a paying job outside the home or volunteer work or bridge clubs. I am cautious about this, though, especially if I had found myself overextended before the relocation. This is an ideal time to enter the mainstream of activity slowly and know when to start saying *no*.

What I usually like to do, since I do not care to be employed outside the home, is to sign up for a class or two at a nearby college. This gets me out of the house a few hours a week, plus gives me something to do *at* home in my spare time. By "spare" I do not mean, as we all know, that I have *nothing* to do, but rather nothing *appealing* to do! Homework for classes, as hard as it is for my children to understand, is enjoyable to me, and striving for good grades gives me a feeling of accomplishing something tangibly worthwhile. In fact, I'll take homework over housework any day!

This may not fulfill your needs or desires, but it is only one of many opportunities available. There are jobs, full-time or part-time. There are classes offered at many places on everything from ceramics to yoga to typing. There are many volunteers needed at hospitals, schools and churches. For the athletically inclined, there are bowling, golf, tennis and racquetball leagues. I have only scratched the surface of available activities, but I think that you can see that my point is to get yourself involved in *something*. It is vital that you settle in your new area as if it's going to be forever, even if you know there is another move in your future.

It is time once again to mention *attitude*. It can make or break you. In fact, nothing can contribute as much to un-happiness in your new home as can a negative attitude. In my discussions with my moved friends and acquaintances, I have come across some who are still unhappy after months (even years) in a new home. Almost without exception, these people have a very negative attitude, and they are usually depending on someone *else*—their spouses, children, friends, anyone but *themselves*—to rescue them from their unhap-piness. Since I have never had the guts to tell them face-to-face to shape up, let me address myself right now to them and any other of you would-be negatives out there.

All right, shape up! Sure, if you say it enough—"I'm just not happy here. I don't have anything to do, and I don't have any friends."—you'll begin to believe it. Before you know it, it will be true!

I remember the woman I met at the doctor's office. We started talking and found we had both lived in the area just two months. When I asked, "How do you like it here?" I was surprised when I got an earful of negative comments. It seems, she whined, that "none of the neighbors have invited us over. They say 'hi' if they see us outside, but that's it." Upon further questioning, I learned that *she* hadn't extended any invitations, either. More about this in a later chapter.

I also remember the gal who was transferred to a different time zone, and she was so against the move that she kept her clocks set at the time of her hometown! How anyone could function an hour off is beyond me. The lady needed help. And I don't mean with her clocks. I mean with her *attitude*.

How is yours?

CHECKLIST

Upon Arrival at New Home

Make any arrangements for services that weren't done before move.

Get safe deposit box.

File claim for losses or damages incurred in move as soon as possible.

Complete Move-in Process.

After Completion of Move-in Process

Get driver's license and car license plates.

Organize taxes.

Get reacquainted with each other.

Explore new territory.

Do the things on your list of Things to Do When Moved and Bored.

Get involved!

7

CHILDREN: RELOCATION WITHOUT DISLOCATION

It is my opinion that the children usually have the least to gain from a move to a new area. Oh sure, we have rationalized each time that it is a good experience for the kids and that it will help them adjust to the many changes that life brings. Like all rationalizations, there is truth to this. Without a lot of tender loving care, attention, and guidance, however, a move can be a great trauma for a child. I have seen at least one child who I feel may have been deeply, if not irreparably, hurt by her untimely and ill-handled move.

Helping Your Kids Adjust

I'm not trying to scare you. Well, yes I am. If you give this some careful thought before you move, deciding just what each child might need to help him or her adjust, you can all but eliminate the potential danger of a relocation and make it the positive experience we rationalized it can be. As in everything else, each child will be different and have different needs, so plan accordingly.

Our first move was much harder on our oldest daughter than we could ever have imagined it would be. "She's only in second grade," I said to my husband when we were wondering how the children would accept the news of the possibility of our first transfer. "She'll be delighted," I assured him, remembering how thrilled I had been every time my father had been transferred (every time until my senior year in high school, that is, as you will hear about later).

As kids so often have a way of doing, however, Kerri proved to be different from me, and she was *not* delighted to hear of the prospect of a move. It meant she had to leave behind a lifelong friend, and they truly did have a remarkable friendship such as some *never* know. I think this type of problem is one of the hardest to solve, because, as Kerri so astutely pointed out, "I'll never be able to replace Debbie!"

We did our best to ease her through this pain, mainly by what we hoped were comforting words. For one thing, we assured her that friends are *not* replaceable and that we would never try to deceive her that they were.

"However," I told her, "there are many more friends out there, perhaps just as special in a different way, and you will have them in addition to, not instead of, Debbie. Plus, Debbie, as well as a lot of our other friends, is apt to be moving one day too, so it would be useless on our part to stay put in the hope that we can all always be happily together."

We discussed mixed emotions again and encouraged all our children to dwell on the positive emotions evoked by the move. We were always able to find several bright spots in each relocation for each individual member of the family, and even Kerri had her happy, excited moments about the move.

But she still missed Debbie. She awoke several times during the first two weeks after our first move, crying because she had dreamed of Debbie. That made her miss her even more, she reported mournfully. What could I say? I was having identical problems missing my friends! And *I* didn't have my parents with me!

We were fortunate, though, that our first move had not taken us too terribly far from "home," so we were able to return for frequent week-end visits, thus weaning ourselves away. This made for a better transition for all of us, and our subsequent moves have not required so much coddling.

We let Kerri have a good cry whenever she seemed to feel the need, even though it broke our hearts, and then proceeded to help her get involved in her new area. Unfortunately, since I had not read this book, we had bought a house in a two-block area that was isolated from the rest of the town by two busy highways. This particular two-block area had a very short supply of children her age. I had to make a special effort to befriend anyone who had a daughter in Kerri's age group and to drive her anywhere that she might have a friend.

The Kerri/Debbie problem turned out to be fairly short-lived, as Kerri's tears soon turned into a "mere" longing for Debbie. (They are, however, still best, though long-distance, friends.) This has really been our only major problem with the children in our moves—and when you take three children times three moves, that makes nine possibilities for problems. One out of nine ain't bad!

School-Associated Problems

There were, of course, other minor challenges. For instance, we moved between Jack's second and third grades. His old school was still printing in second grade, whereas the kids at the new school had learned cursive handwriting in second grade. That made Jack the only third-grader printing his schoolwork. This was easily remedied by a few practice sessions at home and a very patient teacher.

Do be sure to let a teacher know, if you have moved in the summer, that your child is new to the school system. It is, of course, quite apparent when you move in mid-year, but at the beginning of the year it may not be called to the teacher's attention in the mad shuffle of those first days of school. The teacher may have no idea why your son doesn't even know where the lunchroom is!

Also, be sure to let the teachers know, *whenever* you move in, that you want to be made aware of any areas in which your child may be behind so that you and the teacher and the child can all work together to overcome the deficiency as soon as possible. Follow up with frequent notes, calls and visits. In fact, volunteer to help in some capacity at the school if you have the time (maybe you should *make* the time), since there is no better way for the principal and teachers to get to know you and your children—and to know them is to love them, right?

Another potential problem in this area is that your child may be ahead of, not behind, the new class. As so many schools and teachers group the students according to ability in subjects like math and reading, it is easy in a move for your child to be "misplaced" and end up learning the same material twice. If you question a placement, do not hesitate to talk to the teacher about a change.

This happened when Sharon's daughter entered fifth grade at a new school. "Her records had not yet followed her there, and when given a placement test, she seemed momentarily to forget (what with the summer vacation) how to do division problems. Easy to do when you're in fifth grade and have so many more important things on your mind, right?" Sharon chuckled. "At any rate, Maureen was chagrined when she told me about it that night, but after a quick example from me, was able to do even a few difficult division problems. I had a little chat with her teacher, and Maureen was given another placement test and subsequently put in the proper math group." Much valuable learning time could have been wasted had not Maureen communicated with her mother or had her mother not communicated with the teacher, proving that all communication channels in a relocation must be kept open and active.

This experience also points up the need of a little at-home refresher the week before school starts if you have moved during the summer. Usually when you are staying at the same school, complete records will help guide the placement of your children well before the beginning of the school year. It is not always this simple if your children are entering a different school and their records are not entering with them.

For this reason, do try to take the records with you so that you can deliver them promptly to the new school. As the above problem no doubt illustrated, Sharon did not do this when they moved, relying instead on the old school to mail them. It did not make for the best possible transition.

Summer Moves

I have one more thing to say about moving kids during the summer—DON'T. We had only one summer move, and it did turn out surprisingly well because we happened to move to a lake area that abounded in summer activities. It also had kids coming out of the woodwork of every house. Or so it seemed. Had we moved to our other two locations during the summer, I know our children would have been long lonely. The friends and activities they acquired in those towns came about through school, and they were at home in no time because we moved in November. Everyone knew they were new, and they were made to feel quite special as the new kids in school. They were invited to join the Brownies, Cub Scouts, and such—for which I will be forever grateful! Because I *was* worried.

> *11/3/75*
>
> I registered the kids in school. It seemed like such a friendly atmosphere there that I was relieved of some of my anxiety. The kids were quite shy, I could tell, about entering their classrooms. I am sure it is hard for *anyone*, let alone children who have grown up in the safe cocoon of familiar faces, to walk into a room of thirty strangers! Egad! Maybe I'm *not* the one this move is hardest on! At any rate, the teachers seemed very nice and helpful, and the kids had good reports for me after school about their day.

I think many people have the mistaken idea that they are doing their children a favor by waiting until the end of a school year to move. More often than not, I am afraid they are giving their children three months of loneliness. I think it is easier to deal with academic problems that may arise from a change of schools in mid-year than it is to deal with a child's loneliness and boredom.

Getting Your Kids Involved

I strongly suggest getting your children, if they are old enough, into any activities they have even the slightest interest in. This will serve several purposes. It will keep them busy, hence less time to be lonely. It will also automatically expose them to new people, probably of their own age and interests, and people are the stuff that makes friends! And—bonus!—it will expose you to other mothers and fathers who, contrary to popular opinion, are people too and therefore potential friends for you. More about that in the next chapter.

From the last few paragraphs, you may have got the idea that you are better off in a move if you have no children or at least no children past infancy who would be susceptible to bad side effects. Not true! In fact, if you are being relocated, and if you do have elementary school-age children, get down on your knees and give thanks.

From my own experience, as well as from my interviews with others who have moved, I have learned that *nothing* helps the wife to become more firmly and quickly established in the new locale than having children of school age to transport here and there and to watch at athletic events and to call home from the neighbor's. The only thing that comes close for the woman is a career that keeps her happy and busy. This, however, seems to be more rare. So, for all the worry your children ages five to thirteen may cause you, it is well worth it in terms of helping you to keep busy and meet people. And, if handled well, it *will* be a good experience for them.

A word about older children. They're not so easy. In fact, they rarely can be considered an asset in a relocation, since they usually are very reluctant to move once they have started high school. As with the younger children, encourage them to get involved and keep the lines of communication open. Show them that you care! It is quite hard for them to adjust, as a rule, at this particular time in life, which is already filled with the trials and tribulations of young adulthood. Of course, it helps if they're a star quarterback or a double for Bo Derek.

The further along a child is in high school, the harder it is to convince him or her that a relocation would be fun, exciting, and educational. So for those of you with sons or daughters just ready to start their senior year—or perhaps already into it—let me suggest an alternative—something my parents unselfishly did for me when my father was transferred at the beginning of my senior year. What they did enabled me to continue my cheerleading career as well as attend the senior banquet and all the other special events that I just knew I could not live without.

Perhaps, as my parents did, you can make arrangements for your soon-to-be-graduating offspring to stay with friends or relatives to finish the senior year. If it helps you to accept it psychologically, just remind yourself that it's just like him or her going off to college, only a few months earlier.

You can get around the great expense of having to pay tuition, since your child would no longer be considered a resident, by having the friends or relatives named legal guardians. The legal fee for this is nothing compared to what the tuition would be.

Whatever their ages, your children may need your help in making friends. Maybe the best help would be to set a good example. The next chapter is devoted to that art.

CHECKLIST

Throughout the Move
Talk to your children.
More importantly, listen *to your children.*
Plan accordingly.

At the Time of the Move
Take children's school records with you.

As Soon as Possible after the Move

   Talk to the teachers in the new school.
   Study your children's schoolwork for possible mis-
      placement.
   Help your children get involved.

8

"THERE ARE NO STRANGERS, ONLY FRIENDS WE HAVEN'T MET"

Friends are important. And since you probably can't take yours with you when you move, you will need to make some new ones.

From my suggestions in previous chapters, you already have a good idea how to meet people—through work, schools, churches, volunteer organizations and the neighborhood. After meeting these people, how do you turn the ones you like into friends? Well, it takes time—time to have a lot of talks, whereby you reveal your inner selves and past experiences, and time to share new experiences together. "How much time?" you wonder. A year should be plenty of time to turn a casual acquaintance into a good friend. If you have a strong common interest or spend a great deal of time together, it can happen much faster.

Before you even need to worry about the time, though, you better worry about *initiative*. It takes initiative. As much as you may prefer having an already old, dear friend, you just can't when you're new to an area. You have to start somewhere sometime, and there's nothing better than the here and now. The place *not* to start is waiting for people to call you. You must muster up the courage to become the initiator.

1/25/76

Well, I made up my mind this morning that it is obvious that if I'm going to have a friend (or—could it be possible—friends), I am going to have to take the initiative. Somehow I have felt, subconsciously at least, that since I am the "new girl in town," people would come to me to make friends. I mean even after the initial cake and hello. I gave this a great deal of thought, remembering back to Minnesota where I was an old-timer. I was often too busy to take time for a newcomer, but I always had the time if they approached me! I decided that the fact that no one here has latched on to me to be their bosom buddy does not mean that I have bad breath or make boring conversation (though I suppose those are possibilities). Rather, I am sure that they (like me in Minnesota) already have very full lives here and many good friends. I'll see if they can't make room for one more.

Thus, I embarked on my first role as initiator. I remember how awkward I felt. I had met Diane at the Company Christmas party shortly after our move. We hit it off beautifully; we discovered we were both about to turn thirty and neither of us was too happy about it. My husband and I taught her and her husband the bump, and we ended up at the Country Kitchen for ham and eggs at 2:00 *a.m.*, still chatting and getting to know one another—and discovering important details like the fact that we were all native Iowans.

Well, that was fine and dandy, and we said good night, promising to get together soon for coffee. I was disappointed when the following week went by and no call came. I became more disappointed with each passing week. Finally, I called Diane to invite her to my house for coffee, and she enthusiastically accepted. One of the dearest friendships of my life was started. When we moved away just two short years later, Diane and I found parting just as hard as if we had been friends a lifetime.

The best way to *make* a friend is to *be* a friend. Trite but true. So don't be like that lady I met in the doctor's office— the one I told you about in Chapter 6. Do not, I repeat *do not*, feel it is the old-timers' place to invite you over first, or drop in, or call. For one thing, in today's mobile society, there just aren't many old-timers around, and a lot of your neighbors may feel like "new," too, and, therefore, be sitting in the house waiting for some kindly soul to approach them. Why don't *you* be that kindly soul?

Also, don't use the clique excuse to avoid initiating a friendship. I am so tired of hearing the word *clique*, which to me is just a negative term for a group of friends (and, chances are, a group that would welcome *new* friends).

If and when it comes time to part with your new friends, you will no doubt be as sad as Diane and I were. But the alternative is not a good one. I am thinking of Lisa, who, after the third heartbreak of a relocation-induced separation from friends, decided not to make any new ones on arrival at her new location. She was to regret that decision later.

"I never spent such a lonely year in my life," she remembers. "And do you know what? It was even more depressing, when we moved from there, *not* to feel sad about leaving. It just seemed to prove that the year had been an utter waste." Lisa has made several more moves since that one, and what with our moves too, we find time to correspond only at Christmas. I am happy to report, though, that she is now a proponent of the better-to-have-loved-and-lost philosophy.

It will help you to make friends if you have a mate who is cooperative about having people over and who will go places with you. My husband does not particularly enjoy socializing with new people, but he has always gone along with any plans I have made in the hope that it would hasten my adjustment. It has, and it has also given *him* many good friends across the country.

I feel, as I said before, that it is also your responsibility to help your children secure friends, if they seem to be needing help. Most of the time this will probably not be necessary, but be watchful and take appropriate action if it is. Encourage your children to invite friends over and to visit others.

Be brave, take the initiative, and *so what* if you get rebuffed (which, by the way, has yet to happen to me). If you do, try someone else who appeals to you and start establishing that friendship *today*.

CHECKLIST

As Soon as Possible after the Move
  Take the initiative.
  Invite someone over.
  Make a friend!

EPILOGUE

I hope I have given you some practical guidance to help you through your move(s). You may wonder how I feel in retrospect about having moved—since hindsight is always so good.

Well, so far the end to all our relocation stories is another relocation and thus a new beginning. Yes, it seems we are no sooner settled in our home, schools, and community, and can boast of friendships rather than mere acquaintances, than my husband comes home with the now-familiar announcement, "I have something serious to discuss with you, Patty."

And do you know what? It has become downright addictive to all five of us. Whereas we felt practically devastated at the mention of our first transfer, when we hear of one now, our eyes light up as we anticipate all of the excitement and adventure ahead of us.

I am sure the day will come when some or all of us will no longer want to keep branching out but rather will desire to put down roots and grow in one place. I am sure that one day soon we will do just that. In the meantime, we will have had the opportunity to get to know and love many precious people and places.

Who knows? Maybe someday we'll meet you!

117

TIMETABLE

30 Days before Move (sooner if possible)
Start eliminating any food or other items you don't want to move.
If renting, give notice.
Make arrangements with van line.
Complete change-of-address notifications.
Stop writing checks on old accounts.

3 Weeks before Move
Have all records transferred or obtain them to take yourself.
  Medical
  Dental
  School
  Church
Make arrangements for insurance coverage changes.
Make travel plans and get necessary motel reservations.

2 Weeks before Move
Return borrowed items.
Arrange to disconnect or discontinue services.
  Milk
  Cleaners

119

Utilities (if house if sold)
Water (if house is sold)
Phone
Newspaper
Garbage
Water Softener
Arrange to start services in new location.
Utilities
Phone
Water
Newspaper
Garbage
Make arrangements to have appliances serviced for move.

1 Week before Move
Dispose of flammables.
Pack suitcases.
Close bank accounts and transfer funds.
Make up cartons with items to keep with you during move.
Remove pictures and hangings from wall, and spackle and
touch up paint as necessary.

Day before Moving
Clean and air out refrigerator and freezer.
Unplug television.
Clean and air out range.
Finish personal packing.

Moving Day
Clean house.
Ask movers for final cost so you can have payment ready at
destination.
Go with movers for weigh in, if possible.
Check all closets and cupboards.
Dispose of garbage.

Winterize home, if necessary.
Set thermostat.
Shut off faucets.
Turn off lights.
Shut and lock all windows and doors.
Leave keys.

Upon Arrival at New House
Notify van line.
*File claim for losses or damages incurred in move as soon as
    possible.*

GLOSSARY

Appraisal: the estimated value of property as determined by a qualified appraiser.

Appraiser: a person knowledgeable and trained in matters of real estate who is qualified to estimate the value of property.

Asking price: the price at which you are advertising your property for sale—usually high enough to leave room for negotiations via offer and counteroffer.

Assumable mortgage: a mortgage loan that can be transferred to the purchaser, who then becomes responsible for making the payments. The interest rate may or may not remain the same.

Bill of lading: a list of the goods shipped.

Closing: the execution of documents to transfer ownership of property.

Closing costs: the costs to the purchaser and seller to execute the transfer of property and granting of a loan (title search, transfer taxes, insurance, loan-origination fees).

Commission: the percentage of the sales price that the realtor is paid for selling the property.

Contingency: a stipulation or condition on which the sale hinges (e.g., if the earnest-money contract states that the sale is contingent on the purchaser obtaining a mortgage, then the purchaser will be released from the contract and his money refunded if he is unable to obtain a mortgage).

Contract: a written agreement.

Contract for deed: a written agreement, also called a *land contract*, whereby the buyer pays the seller directly all or part of the purchase price instead of obtaining a loan through a lending institution. This is done in installments over a specified number of years, with the title remaining with the seller.

Conventional loan: a mortgage loan not insured by the government.

Counteroffer: a new selling price offered by the seller after receiving an initial offer from a prospective buyer.

Deed: written under seal, this document conveys the title of real property from one party to another.

Deposit: this is the earnest money paid to the seller to bind the sales agreement.

Down payment: the amount of money the buyer must pay toward the purchase of the house, not counting the mortgage.

Earnest money: money paid by the purchaser to show his intent to buy and to hold the property for him.

Earnest-money contract: the formal written agreement between the prospective buyer and the seller, stipulating that the buyer has agreed to buy and the seller has agreed to sell the property for a specified price. This contract includes any contingencies and states a deadline for closing.

Equity: the value of the property minus the amount still owed on the mortgage.

Escrow: money deposited with a neutral third party by the two parties involved, to be paid under certain conditions.

Exclusion: for our purposes, this refers to a prospective buyer named in the listing agreement with the realtor. If said buyer purchases the home, no commission would be paid to the realtor.

FHA: a government-insured loan that requires less down payment but higher closing costs.

Financing: the method by which the buyer will obtain money to purchase a house.

GI loan: a government-insured loan available to veterans of military service. It usually requires no down payment.

Interest rate: the annual percentage of the loan balance that is charged for a loan.

Land contract: see *contract for deed*.

Lease with option to buy: a written agreement between owner and renter that stipulates that if the renter decides to buy the property by a specified date at a specified price, the rent paid up to that point will be applied toward the purchase.

Listed: this term refers to the fact that a home is for sale.

Listing agreement: a written contract between seller and realtor that stipulates that if the house is sold during a certain specified period of time, the realtor will receive a specified percentage of the sales price for performing his services.

Listing sheet: a reference sheet that realtors, and some owners who are offering the house for sale by themselves, furnish. It gives information about the house, including such pertinent facts as price, taxes, room dimensions, and any extras.

Loan-origination fee: the percentage of the loan that is charged by the lending institution for the making of the loan.

Market: potential buyers for a house; also, available homes listed for sale.

Market value: the monetary worth of your home based on the recent sales prices of nearby and comparable homes.

Monthly payment: the amount of money a homeowner must pay each month for the house, including principal, interest, and sometimes taxes and insurance.

Mortgage: a loan for the purpose of purchasing a house, using the house as collateral.

Mortgagee: the lender of a mortgage loan.

Multiple-listing service: a service through which member realtors can show and sell property listed with other members of the service.

Net realized selling price: the amount the seller receives after paying closing costs, realtor's commission, attorney's fees, fixing-up expenses, etc.

Offer: the amount of money a prospective buyer proposes, in writing, to pay the seller for the property.

Open house: a specific, advertised time, usually for two or three hours on a Sunday afternoon, during which any interested parties may tour the house without appointment or prior arrangements.

Pending assessments: taxes or other obligations due on a property.

Points: a point represents 1 percent of the mortgage. See also *loan-origination fee.*

Possession date: the date by which the previous owners must have vacated the premises so that the new owners may move in.

Power of attorney: a legal maneuver by which one signs over authorization for another person to act in one's behalf.

Principal: the outstanding balance on a loan.

Promissory note: a signed document used in lieu of a cash payment saying a certain amount of money is owed by one party to another.

Purchase agreement: see *earnest-money contract.*

Purchase price: the price the buyer pays for a house.

Real-estate broker: an individual who has a valid real-estate broker's license and can provide the necessary services to accommodate the sale of real estate.

Real-estate salesman: an individual who is employed by a real-estate broker to provide the services of a broker but only under direct supervision of the licensed real-estate broker.

Realtor: a real-estate broker associated with the National Association of Realtors.

Security deposit: the amount paid by a renter that is refunded when he moves if there has been no damage to the rented property.

Selling price: the amount of money for which a house is sold.

Title: the means by which the owner has legal possession of his property.

Title insurance: a contract that insures against defects in titles to real-estate property.

VA: an agency of the federal government that insures mortgage loans for veterans.

INDEX